BEYOND THE SEA
a Wren at War

CHRISTIAN LAMB

MARDLE

First published in 2021 by Mardle Books
15 Church Road
London, SW13 9HE
www.mardlebooks.com

Text © 2021 Christian Lamb

Paperback ISBN 9781914451027
eBook ISBN 9781914451119

A CIP catalogue record for this book is available from the British Library.

Every reasonable effort has been made to trace copyright-holders of material
reproduced in this book, but if any have been inadvertently overlooked
the publishers would be glad to hear from them.

Typeset by Danny Lyle
Printed in the UK

10 9 8 7 6 5 4 3 2 1

Cover image: Alamy – Sir Cecil Beaton

PRAISE FOR CHRISTIAN LAMB

'True character, very funny and idiosyncratic'
Sir Roy Strong, Hon. D. Litt, Ph.D., FSA, FRSL.

'Fabulously eccentric Christian Lamb: marvellously funny, indomitable, charming and with the swagger of a musketeer'
Tim Smit, CBE, Chief Executive of the Eden Project

To my daughter Felicity Rollo who, in spite of
her busy life and large family, finds time and takes
enormous trouble to arrange wonderful treats for me,
which are always a lovely surprise.

Christian with Felicity, 1945

D-DAY REMEMBERED

On June 6 2019, I was invited to Portsmouth to celebrate the 75th anniversary of D-Day, that famous day which marked the start of Operation Overlord, the vastly complicated mission that was to bring about the beginning of the end of the Second World War.

I joined 6,000 guests, drawn from serving members of the armed forces, international dignitaries and veterans, to hear Her Majesty The Queen give a speech of thanks. Flanked by her son the Prince of Wales and President Donald Trump of the United States of America, the Queen first observed that when she attended the commemoration of the 60th anniversary of D-Day, some thought it might be the last such celebration. I'm sure many of the veterans in attendance were in accord when she said, "But the wartime generation – my generation – is resilient, and I am delighted to be with you in Portsmouth today."

The Queen remembered the many hundreds of thousands of soldiers, sailors and airmen, from all the Allied nations, who set forth from Britain to northern France in the early hours of that long-ago June day, saying, "In a broadcast to the nation at that time, my Father, King George VI, said: '…what is demanded from us all is something more than courage and endurance; we need a revival of spirit, a new unconquerable resolve…' That is exactly what those brave men brought to the battle, as the fate of the world depended on their success."

As Her Majesty spoke, I recalled my own small role in the famous operation to take the beaches of northern France and start the Allied pushback into Europe.

In early 1944, as a third officer WRNS at the age of 23, I was posted to the Combined Operations Headquarters in Whitehall. There, in a tiny office beneath the stairs, while Churchill himself took meetings on the upper floors, I was set to work. It was a top-secret task that I could not discuss, even with my naval officer husband. All I knew at the time was that it was of vital importance that I should be accurate. Lives might depend on my work.

In 2019 the Queen acknowledged the many men who did not return from the battle to wrest northern France from the Nazis, saying, "The heroism, courage and sacrifice of those who lost their lives will never be forgotten."

Listening to her moving speech, I nodded in agreement. Victory in World War Two required the hard work and sacrifice of many millions of people, and I felt glad to have been able to play my part.

That day in Portsmouth reminded me that those of us who were old enough to serve in the war dwindle in number with each passing year. For that reason, it feels more important than ever to share my memories of that time and to pass on the experiences of my husband John, my friends and my fellow Wrens.

EARLY DAYS

As I begin to write this book, the United Kingdom is in a third lockdown to contain the coronavirus pandemic. Being locked down, unable to leave the house for anything but essential purposes, has been a mixed blessing. While I've missed spending time with my family and friends and being able to travel freely, having nothing much to do has given me the space to reflect upon a century of life and the adventures I've had along the way.

I was born in 1920, just as Europe was emerging from another pandemic. The devastation of the First World War was swiftly followed by the so-called Spanish Flu. A third of the world's population was infected by the H1N1 virus between 1918 and 1920. Then, as now, large gatherings were banned and the wearing of masks became commonplace – but the virus still claimed millions of lives.

I was the second of two daughters born to Rear-Admiral Ronald Wolseley Oldham OBE and Ethel Oldham (née Berry). My parents were both born in India. My father came from a naval family and he himself joined the Royal Navy at just 12 years old, when he became a student at the naval training school HMS *Britannia*, in Portsmouth.

Papa became an expert in navigation and went on to command a number of battleships, including HMS *Revenge* and HMS *Nelson*. During the First World War he fought at Gallipoli when the 'Entente' powers –the British Empire, France and Russia – tried to take control of the Turkish Straits. The Ottoman Empire was allied with Germany.

The campaign was a disaster, which led to a terrible loss of life, remembered in Australia and New Zealand each year on ANZAC day. I remember my father telling me with characteristic under-statement that at Gallipoli he had been sunk three times in one day without getting his feet wet.

My parents had three children altogether: me, my sister Anne and, eight years after I was born, my younger brother Francis. At the time of my birth, they were living in Scotland. I don't remember much about those early days. Before I was very old, we moved south of the border to London.

One of the first memories I recall from that time, going back as far as I can, was sitting up, facing my sister Anne, being pushed in our large double pram. There was barely a year between Anne and me so we were like twins; she was always my favourite relation. I must have been about three, and we were being taken by our nanny up Victoria Road, W8 to the Broad Walk in Kensington Gardens. The pram's hoods were up because it was raining.

For years after, I was often teased because an occupation I apparently enjoyed on these outings was eating my straw hat. This may have had something to do with my pet rabbit which lived outside our nursery window on an extension to the balcony. Here I could safely go and feed him with all his favourite treats, including straw, perhaps?

I also have a vivid recollection of the day – I was about six by then – when I was suddenly able to read. The jumble of letters laid out on mats on the floor had for ever seemed despairingly impenetrable, until that unforgettable instant when they made sense.

Anne was much cleverer and quicker than me and was never without a book – even when bending down to do up her shoes, she would have a book open on the floor beside her. My mother tried to make me into a bookworm as well, giving me all sorts of suitable titles to tempt me, but for a long time I would only read one book over and over again. It was called *A Fairy to Stay*.

I was regaling a friend of mine about this book the other day and when she looked it up on her telephone (the fount of all knowledge these days), she found it was for sale at £200. I told this story to my son-in-law David Rollo, when to my amazement he said, "I will give it to you for your 100th birthday!"

I was so thrilled and when it arrived exactly on my birthday, I started to read it again. Imagine my astonishment to find that, despite having read it so often as a child, I did not remember what happened. I spent the next day reading it without interruption until I finished it and discovered the end plot. It was such a pleasure, I can't tell you!

I won't forget the exciting moment a few years later, when Anne and I found two shiny new bicycles hidden (several weeks in advance of Christmas Day) in the dining room cupboard. After receiving these wonderful presents, we used to ride them daily from 12 Eldon Road, W8, where we lived, to the nearby Convent of the Assumption in Kensington Square. The school was run on the Montessori method, a system of educating young children invented by Doctor Maria Montessori, which involved clay-modelling, mat-plaiting and such forms of self-discipline. It also included learning multiplication tables and many other things by heart, which trained the memory – a valuable start – essential and taken for granted in those days.

Bicycling to school we used to pass the post office, called Turner's, where we often purchased sweets by putting the cost (until she discovered it) onto our mother's account. One day Anne knocked into an old lady on our way home. This was observed by our papa who happened to be walking on the other side of the square. He simply pretended not to know us!

Having learnt to read at the convent in Kensington Square, my education progressed via many changes, taking in a sojourn in Malta, where we followed my father, who was appointed captain of HMS *Shropshire* in June 1929. HMS *Shropshire* was a County-class cruiser, part of the First Cruiser Squadron of the British Mediterranean Fleet. The Mediterranean Fleet was one of the most important squadrons of the Royal Navy at that time, protecting the sea links between Britain and its eastern Empire. It had been based in Malta since 1800.

I will never forget (although I was only about 10), seeing His Majesty's Fleet come in to Malta's Grand Harbour. I stood on the breakwater and watched battleships, battlecruisers, cruisers, destroyers, corvettes and innumerable other ships sailing into this most beautiful of destinations. It was a sight to see! Those were the days when we had the finest fleet in the world. Perhaps it was at that moment that I fell a little in love with the idea of the naval life.

FOLLOWING THE FLEET

It is interesting to note that in the 1930s naval families were not provided with accommodation or transport to 'Follow the fleet', but if they wished, had to do so at their own expense.

We travelled out to Malta by P&O Liner: my mother, sister and small brother, and our governess Enid de Vere, whose father was the chief of police on the island. Enid was engaged to teach Anne and me, and to look after my brother. Also, when we arrived, she found a class of other children who were keen to join in. As well as her teaching duties, Enid had a lot of spare time and used it to collect young men, of which there were plenty… But she was somewhat over-enthusiastic and caused a great many of them to retreat to their ships and batten down the hatches.

Our voyage to Malta was quite eventful. As we came to the Bay of Biscay, we encountered a tremendous storm. Nearby, a smaller vessel found itself in difficulties, so our captain diverted our ship to help. For the duration of the storm, we sailed round and round the smaller vessel to protect it from the raging seas, until such time as it could continue safely on its way. Of course, sailing like this made most of our passengers sea-sick, but Anne and I had strong stomachs and were unbothered by the storm or the endless circling. Each day we would be the only two people at meals.

Malta, though only 14 miles long, is strategically placed to command the channels between the southern extremity of Europe and the northern coast of Africa; thus it had been fought over through the centuries by the Phoenicians, the Carthaginians, the Romans, the Normans and the Turks. Hannibal was born there, St Paul was shipwrecked on the island (hence St Paul's Bay) and in 1798 Napoleon occupied it.

However, in 1799 the British captured it and in 1814 it was confirmed as being under British rule by the Treaty of Paris and remained so until 1963, when it became an independent nation. So for 150 years it was the main naval base for the British Mediterranean Fleet and famous for its multitudinous bells, smells and yells.

Luckily Malta was amazingly cheap in those days and so we were able to live in a lovely house called Upway Villa, in Guardamangia. Our house was opposite the Villa Guardamangia, which was at the time leased to Lord Mountbatten and would later be home to Princess Elizabeth and Prince Philip in the early years of their marriage. We had a live-in domestic staff and even a chauffeur called Edward, though he did have bare feet.

Life in Malta was especially memorable to us children for the riding lessons we had at the Marsa, the polo club. Here we proceeded early in the morning, when it was cool, fetched in a *carozzi* – a horse drawn vehicle – to have our lessons on the racecourse. The horse upon which I learned to ride was called 'Far Tatton'. He went on to have a more distinguished career as David Niven's polo pony.

Of course, David Niven was not a famous film star then, but a humble subaltern in the Highland Light Infantry, a Scottish infantry regiment – and not the most exciting regiment in the British Army. In fact, Niven joked in his memoirs that upon graduating from Sandhurst, he had asked to be assigned to the Argyll and Sutherland Highlanders or the Black Watch, before putting down as his third choice "anything but the Highland Light Infantry." His antipathy to the HLI apparently sprang from the fact that they wore tartan trousers, rather than kilts.

Niven spent a couple of years in Malta, mostly using the time to improve his polo and rugby skills, but he ultimately found peace-time army life far too dull and left the HLI in 1933 to pursue his acting dream. He quickly became very successful and might have sat out World War Two in a Hollywood mansion; the day after Britain declared war on Germany in 1939, however, he travelled back to Britain and rejoined the army, this time as a lieutenant in the Rifle Brigade. Boredom set in again, however, and he got himself transferred to the Commandos, which better suited his dashing style. He also worked with the army Film and Photographic Unit, which would play an important role in the lead up to D-Day.

One expedition I remember from this time in Malta was when my parents decided to take us to Sicily. This was a great excitement, as it meant travelling by sea for two or three days. During the trip we encountered a terrific Mediterranean storm – quite unpredictable, but to which the area was well known to be prone. We had to lie off the coast of Sicily for two days, in this rough sea, quite unable to land on the island.

When we did eventually land, we made straight for the famous volcano, Mount Etna, which was the exciting place my parents wanted to visit. They had shown us a graphic picture of it erupting which I have never forgotten, and as our hotel was within range of the summit, you could see the smouldering crater in the distance and imagine it bursting into flames and the whole trembling garden, from where we were gazing, disintegrating right where we were standing.

Some of the other activities we were indulged in as children were the parties on many of the ships based in Malta. The sailors loved dressing up as pirates and giving us rides in the lifts which were intended for taking ammunition up to the 12-inch guns.

We also practised swimming and diving in the sea and at the Tigne Swimming Club, in Sliema, on what seemed a very high diving board then. Many years later, when I saw it again, it seemed to have shrunk... We also had Highland dancing lessons and ballet, and on one occasion gave a performance at the Opera House in Valletta, which started at nine o'clock at night – what emancipation!

Life in Malta was quite enjoyable for us children and we were very disappointed to have to leave.

BACK TO SCHOOL

Having spent just over two years in Malta, in September 1931, we returned to England and lived in London again, while Papa, an admiral by now, was based at the Admiralty.

This was a sad period in our lives, when our parents broke up. It was mostly my mother's problems with money that were the cause of it all. She had no idea how to control her spending and Papa was not used to having Harrods banging on his front door! It wasn't only Harrods. My mother bought our clothes from a most expensive shop in Sloane Street called Hayford's, which had a Royal Warrant for dressing the children at Buckingham Palace.

With our parents now separated, our mother had to change her shopping habits. We also had to move house again. This time to Sussex.

Our father's mother Norah, whom we referred to as 'Brighton Granny', was one of three sisters – Norah, Ella and Amy Haig. They were first cousins of the famous Field Marshal Douglas Haig, who commanded the British Expeditionary Force on the Western

Front during the First World War. Haig was a national hero, who had devoted himself to the welfare of ex-servicemen in the years after the war and founded the British Legion. Many of those ex-servicemen had thronged the streets of London to pay their respects at his 1928 funeral.

Since separating from our mother, Papa had spent his leave with Brighton Granny at her rather nice house called Parkhurst, in High Hurstwood, near Uckfield in Sussex. So that Papa could come and see us during our school holidays, our mother rented a cottage nearby.

Papa would come over in his rather grand car – I seem to remember he always had a Rolls or something like that – and we would all go off to lunch somewhere. I particularly recall how we would circle a roundabout several times while we discussed where we would go. When we were all agreed, he would take us wherever and expressed great interest in our choice of menu, always insisting that we had our absolute favourites and several puddings if we could fit them in.

He never forgot our birthdays, but instead of presents he would send us generous cheques, so we had the pleasure of choosing what we really wanted.

Other times, Papa would come and take us to visit his mother. Occasionally her sisters, Amy and Ella, would be there as well. On one occasion there was tapioca for pudding and if there is one pudding in the world I could not face it was this. I sat there with tears trickling down my face, which they all thought most entertaining. Luckily Papa rescued me and I was able to regain my equilibrium.

We did not see a great deal of Brighton Granny, but we did discover that she and her sisters were all enthusiastic spiritualists and enjoyed many seances with some rather well-known mediums in London.

Spiritualism had become very popular in the 1920s as people were keen to be able to talk to loved ones who had died during the war, or in the Spanish Flu pandemic that followed hot on its heels. There was barely a family in Britain that had not been touched by tragedy, and a great many found comfort in the idea that those dear to them might still be able to communicate from beyond. Spiritualism provided hope this was possible.

When as children we listened to the Haig sisters recalling their encounters with the spirits of the dead, we were always rather surprised at what they had thought worth discussing. We were amazed that such trivial subjects as the rearrangement of furniture or what colour a new carpet might be, seemed to preoccupy the dead far more than the whereabouts of a lost will or document, which you might think rather more important.

Not long after our parents' separation, our maternal grandparents also became involved in our upbringing.

Our mother's mother – Scotch Granny, as she was known – was brought up by her Calder parents in Scotland. My great-grandfather, Uncle Jack as we called him, decided to educate his seven children by teaching them at home for half the year and then taking them all over Europe for the other half of the year to broaden their minds.

My grandmother survived this peripatetic childhood and fell in love at the age of 18 with Frederick Berry, a doctor with the Indian

Civil Service, who had been awarded a Companion of the Order of the Star of India. So Scotch Granny sailed – and at that time this meant really under sail – out to Bombay, suitably chaperoned, and with a number of her relations, to be married in the cathedral there. The young newlyweds then travelled to the remote part of India where Frederick was working.

But their happiness, sadly, was to be short-lived. One day not long after they were married, Frederick came home and told Scotch Granny that because he had been in contact with cholera, he would have to stay away from her. Not long afterwards, he developed the dreaded disease and died. To make things worse, my grandmother was pregnant by this time with my mother. With no relatives nearby and only a local ayah to help her, my grandmother gave birth.

Bravely, Scotch Granny managed to travel back to Bombay with her new baby and subsequently sailed to England. How much sadder she must have felt on this return journey than when she sailed out, full of expectation, to Bombay to be married. My grandmother eventually returned home to Ardargie, the family house near Perth, where her six brothers and sisters were still living. She had been through so much – she'd travelled to India, been married, been widowed and become a mother – and yet she was still barely out of her teenage years.

My grandmother married again 15 years later, so my mother subsequently became elder sister to two half-sisters and a half-brother. She was, however, very specially treated throughout her upbringing – and as a child she had been doted on by my grandmother's younger siblings, her aunts and uncles, which may have accounted for her hopeless attitude to money when she married my father.

With Scotch Granny in charge again, Anne and I were sent to a boarding school – the Assumption Convent in Ramsgate, Kent, which I chiefly remember for the icy wind which seemed to come straight from Siberia, and how I used to run from one radiator to another endeavouring to keep warm. The weather in Kent was very different to that which I had become used to in Malta, and I missed the Mediterranean sun.

The Convent was a Catholic school and many of our fellow pupils were from France and Spain. The Spanish children had been sent overseas to escape the civil war that was tearing their country apart.

My first term at the convent, I was confined to the back row in class, from where I could see nothing, being very short sighted. Anne was very cross with me when I left my classroom and ran into hers complaining that they were trying to make me do things I couldn't! There was also another punishment – a huge field of parsnips, which far too often provided the only vegetables in our diet.

However, I was quite successful at sport at school and was captain of all the hockey and netball teams and enjoyed competitions such as high jump and sprinting. I invented a crafty way of starting in the 100-metre race, which was to listen very closely to the starting gun when instead of pausing as everyone else seemed to do, I took off at once and usually won.

There was a fräulein at the school who taught German, which I did not learn, but I do remember walking down the corridor behind her and wondering at her enormous derrière. She used to sit beside me at the head of my table for meals and I won't forget the day she banged my elbow on the table as punishment for resting it there. I lay in wait until the day arrived when I did the same to her. I was rightly punished for my behaviour but whatever they made me do was well worth the satisfaction of my revenge.

We had rather good lessons in elocution and deportment, which stood me in good stead when many years later (about 50!) I started one of my new careers – lecturing. The day I left the convent I had a long chat with Reverend Mother, whom I was very fond of and I had the temerity to tell her how she could improve her running of the school. If I had been her I would have boxed my ears, but she took it in good humour without necessarily promising to take my advice.

After leaving school, I was sent to France for a year, staying with several different families around the countryside. I was very happy to be overseas and became totally absorbed in becoming bilingual. I read all the riveting French novels which had been banned during my previous life at the convent school (in between falling in and out of love, in French, of course). I loved the French language and found it fascinating to discover the exact meaning of particular words which could not be translated into English. I had the same problem translating some very specific English words into French.

While in France I also had German lessons to prepare me for the next visit, which was to be to a family in Germany. I found the German language very unattractive (prejudice remaining from the elbow-banging fräulein, perhaps?) with its guttural pronunciation and verb always at the end of long sentences.

The last family I stayed with in France was at Mulhouse, near the Vosges mountains and not far from the Swiss and German borders. There were three girls in that family and we had a lovely time exploring the countryside, which was covered in 'myrtie' bushes – myrtle bushes as I knew them. This was a particularly delicious fruit which left your mouth looking completely black.

This continued for six whole months. During that time I managed not to open a single newspaper, so I had no idea what was going on in the outside world. It was very easy to enjoy my life in France and not pay any attention at all to the very inconvenient war which was brewing not all that far away.

OUTBREAK OF WAR

After the end of the First World War, the combatants signed the Treaty of Versailles, which imposed upon Germany a programme of financial reparations to pay for the damage they had caused. At the same time, Germany was subject to a strict policy of disarmament, designed to prevent another war.

These measures, combined with a worldwide depression, were the conditions that gave the Nazi party an opportunity to flourish, as Adolf Hitler promised he could return Germany to greatness. In such difficult times, it was easy for him to persuade the German people that their problems were the fault of enemies from both outside and from within, namely, the Jews.

Unfortunately, many believed him.

As soon as he became Chancellor in 1933, Hitler began the process of rearmament. To begin with, the reaction of the French and British governments was to try to appease him. Indeed, Hitler initially hoped to make an Anglo-German alliance, holding Britain up as an example of successful Aryan imperialism. A great many high-profile British aristocrats and politicians seemed flattered by this idea. The Duke and Duchess of Windsor, the former King Edward VIII and his wife Wallis Simpson, were houseguests of Hitler as late as 1937.

In 1938 however, things began to change when the Nazis annexed Austria and invaded Czechoslovakia, in a move that Hitler claimed was to reunite the Germans living in those countries with their homeland. By 1939, the situation could no longer be ignored. Nazi Germany had signed a pact with the Soviets to divide up Eastern Europe, leaving the way clear for the Nazis to invade Poland.

After the invasion of Czechoslovakia, the British Government had promised to guarantee Poland's sovereignty. If Hitler did invade that country, as seemed to be his plan, then Britain would be drawn into war to honour its promise. As Hitler made preparations to move east, the whole world watched to see what would happen next.

The first I knew about the alarming situation unfolding in Eastern Europe was when I received a telegram from my father, sent to the house in Mulhouse where I had been having such a wonderful time. "War imminent. Come home," was all it said. Though I still did not know the details of the crisis at hand, I knew I could not ignore my father's urgent summons.

I quickly arranged to travel to Dieppe, where I met my mother who was on her way back from the south of France with my small brother. My bulging suitcase chose this moment to burst, so our first action was to buy a new one and repack it in the shop. We then had to get to the port, from where we caught one of the last ferries home to England. The ferry was full of travellers like us, reacting to the news that war now seemed inevitable. The atmosphere on board was tense as we all wondered what lay ahead.

Having returned to England, we travelled up to Scotland, to stay with my maternal grandmother (Scotch Granny), while I decided what to do next.

My Scotch grandparents lived in a lovely house called Blarour, just beside Spean Bridge, from where you could see the Lochaber hills. Anne and I spent part of our summer holidays there every year. My grandmother was a great gardener and it was among her collection of plants that I learnt my first Latin name, that of the ravishing blue Himalayan poppy – *meconopsis betonicifolia var. baileyi*. This turned out to be the beginning of my gardening mania, which developed into a passion for me so much later in my life.

At the front of Blarour was an enormous lawn, starting with a steep hill, down which as small children we had loved to roll. The lawn then spread several hundred yards to where the land dipped sharply and a little footpath ran round the edge and down the hill to join the curving drive and eventually to the big gate which opened nearly on to the bridge itself. The immense lawn had to be mown every week with a horse-drawn machine, which took several hours to accomplish. The valley also provided space for the sheltered garden and was the background to Scotch Granny's heavenly plants.

I had been intending to try for Oxford University – Anne was already there, reading philology, which is the history of language – but I did not have sufficient grades. I had been advised that I could improve the situation by taking an exam of unseen translations, for which I would be tutored from Oxford by correspondence. The final exam was invigilated by the Benedictine Monks of Fort Augustus Abbey who lived in their wonderful monastery beside Loch Ness, not far away. Many of them claimed to have seen the monster. I did get the grades I needed but it soon became clear that university would have to wait.

Hitler invaded Poland on 1 September 1939. Two days later, our Prime Minister Neville Chamberlain addressed the nation over the radio, informing us that the Germans had left us with no choice but to declare war. France and Canada followed suit.

That same day, SS *Athenia*, a passenger liner out of Glasgow, was sunk by a U-boat – an unterseeboot, a German submarine – with 117 passengers and crew killed. Though the Germans denied their involvement in the incident, the headlines in the British press declared "Empire at War". We were all on high alert as we waited for what we thought would be imminent invasion.

I began to absorb the atmosphere around me; as this was so soon after the end of the terrible First World War, it had quite an effect. I was no longer able to avoid the news as I had done during my time in France.

I realised that at 19 I was old enough to do 'my bit'. This meant finding some occupation that would help the war effort. I was very patriotic and knew this was the right thing to do.

DOING MY BIT

My first thoughts were of becoming a nurse with the VAD (Voluntary Aid Detachment) and I started some first aid classes to prepare myself. I practised my bandaging on my long-suffering grandfather's bald head, though it did occur to me that any person who needed care for a head injury would be unlikely to come within my range. By the time it came to learning how to dress stumps, I had decided nursing was not my forte.

I did pick up some other useful skills however. My grandmother had arranged for her chauffeur, who was called Willie, to teach me how to drive. I don't remember what sort of car I took my lessons in but it was quite large. Fortunately, the long driveway enabled me to practise manoeuvres without endangering myself or anyone else until I was ready for the open road.

I also began to learn to play bridge. Among the many friends of my grandparents who came to play was a Colonel Frank Laughton. Once, when he and I were playing as partners, we called and made a Grand Slam, which anyone who has ever played bridge will know is very exciting! Though I did not know it at the time, Colonel

Laughton would come to play a small but quite important role in the next stage of my life.

It was while I was in Spean Bridge that I came to hear about the WRNS – a part of the Royal Navy that women could join. As my father was now an admiral in that historic service, it seemed to be destined that I should become a member. The advertisement which suggested a Wren might free a sailor to go to sea made some sense and the thought of doing something really useful was very attractive.

The Women's Royal Naval Service was originally formed in 1917 under the directorship of Dame Katharine Furse, who had led the British Red Cross Voluntary Aid Detachment stationed in France since the outbreak of the First World War in 1914. Her experience with the Red Cross made her the ideal candidate to help shape the first of the women's armed services. By the end of the war, Furse oversaw some 7,000 Wrens working as cooks, stewards, drivers and in intelligence. Their role was to support the Royal Navy from the land. In fact, the WRNS motto at that time was "Never at Sea".

After the Armistice was signed, the WRNS was disbanded but in the late 1930s, with another war looming, it was decided that it should be revived. That task fell to Vera Laughton Mathews.

A devout Christian from a naval family, Vera Laughton Mathews was a remarkable woman. Her father was the naval historian Sir John Knox Laughton and she studied at King's College London. She was an early proponent of women's rights and an active member of the Women's Political and Social Union and the Catholic Women's Suffrage Society. In 1914, she became the editor of *The Suffragette*. She had joined the Wrens towards the end of the First World War, taking the rank of principal officer (the equivalent of a lieutenant commander in the Royal Navy). She was the Unit Officer of HMS *Victory VI*, the WRNS Training Depot at Crystal Palace in South London, until she was demobbed in 1919.

In the inter-war years, Vera Laughton Mathews continued to devote herself to public service, playing an active role in the Sea Rangers. She captained the Sea Rangers' ship for 10 years from 1928. At the same time she continued to work tirelessly in support of women's rights and was responsible for helping to raise the legal age of marriage to 16.

Now that the WRNS was needed again, Vera Laughton Mathews was the ideal woman for the job of rebuilding it. In 1939, she was appointed as the new director and immediately dedicated herself to her task, working round the clock to reply to the many applications which arrived in response to her advertisements for new recruits.

With former 'chief woman officer' of the Civil Service, Ethel Goodenough, as her second-in-command, Vera Laughton Mathews launched the new WRNS with a minimum of staff, no official training regime and, to begin with, no uniforms. Categories in which new Wrens could serve were still limited and none of them were aboard ship.

Gradually, however, she persuaded the Royal Navy to expand the Wrens' remit. The success of her campaign can be seen in remarks made in parliament by the Civil Lord of the Admiralty, who said, "I have no doubt that if you gave the WRNS half a chance they would be perfectly prepared to sail a battleship."

Vera Laughton Mathews was particularly skilled when it came to dealing with the Admirals of the Royal Navy admirals, several of whom were still of the opinion that women should not be admitted to the 'Senior Service'. She smoothed the way with a mixture of dogged persistence and charm. Among her many achievements was the commissioning of a new WRNS uniform, complete with a splendid tricorn hat. She also persuaded the Admiralty to allow superintendent WRNS to wear four blue stripes. Stripes are very important in the Royal Navy, with many senior officers refusing to deal with anyone they consider to be sporting too few. Vera Laughton Mathews was able to obtain the equivalent stripes of a rear admiral for herself.

It so happened that my bridge friend, Colonel Laughton, was Vera's brother, so he added a reference to my application to join which was a great help.

In the winter of 1939, I duly travelled down to London for my interview at the WRNS headquarters which happened to be just beside Admiralty Arch, over Drummonds Bank in Trafalgar Square. My first encounter with a senior Wren officer, Chief Officer Nancy Osborne, took place there. My qualifications were discussed. These consisted of being bilingual in French and... not much else.

"Can you type?" Chief Officer Osborne asked me.

I could not. However, she offered me a job there and then at the Wrens' HQ. I was much disconcerted by this, as I had not decided to join the WRNS to spend my life working in London among elderly ladies like her. I had envisaged spending time in a port, replacing sailors who could then go to sea. The advertisement I'd responded to had suggested that was the general idea. It exhorted young women to "join the Wrens and free a man for the Fleet".

After the interview, I was sent for a medical, which was quite straightforward, except when it came to the doctor testing my hearing. I told him that as a teenager, I'd had a mastoid operation and, as a result, he decided that I must be deaf. He tested his theory by going to the far end of the room and whispering. At the time, this was the only 'hearing test' available. Fortunately, I was able to hear everything he said. The doctor seemed almost disappointed.

When I politely turned down Chief Officer Osborne's offer of a job at the WRNS HQ, she suggested instead that I could go to the training establishment in Kensington and volunteer to become a coder or writer, which I might prefer.

This sounded much more like it!

So she sent me off to start a most exciting career.

BASIC TRAINING

In January 1940, I began my basic training at Campden Hill Road, Kensington, in a building that had previously belonged to London University. In the age-old tradition of the Royal Navy, administrative buildings were known as 'stone frigates' and named as if they were ships. The Wrens' training facility was named HMS *Pembroke I*.

We shared the building with the FANY (the First Aid Nursing Yeomanry). The FANY, also known as the Princess Royal's Volunteer Corps, was an all-female corps, based along army lines. It had been formed in 1907 to provide a link between battle and field hospitals, with its early members riding to the front line on horses.

In the Second World War, the FANY continued to provide transportation services but also famously worked alongside the SOE, Churchill's Special Operations Executive, as coders and signallers, and also as agents in the field. The SOE's remit was to support the resistance behind enemy lines with espionage and sabotage. The SOE sent 50 women into German-occupied France, of whom 39 were members of the FANY, including the celebrated agent Violette Szabo, whose brave missions were dramatised in the film *Carve Her Name with Pride*.

On my arrival at this joint training facility, I was shown into the head office where I met the Queen Bee herself: Chief Officer Hilda Buckmaster. She was one of Katharine Furse's original recruits, having joined the WRNS from the Red Cross in 1917. She'd had a very exciting life since then. In the 1920s she'd sailed before the mast on one of the last windjammers, the SS *Panape*. She had worked as a deck hand on *Panape*'s voyages between Australia and Finland. More recently, she had been an active member of the Liberal Party.

Chief Officer Buckmaster was a formidable woman of grand stature who put me in mind of a ship's figurehead. On arrival, she greeted me warmly.

"How nice to welcome a breath of fresh sea air!"

This was presumably referring to my father's rank. After a short conversation, she asked me what I wanted to do. "Would you like to volunteer to become a writer? Otherwise, there are a few vacancies for coders…"

I pounced on 'coder' as it sounded interesting and mysterious. I was then given an arm badge and I signed some sort of document which officially made me a member of the WRNS. There were no uniforms as yet. Finally, a fellow Wren led me to my quarters and started to give me the low down on what it was all about.

On the way to the bedrooms, which were referred to as cabins, we visited various training places where physical training (PT), typing and shorthand, cooking etc were underway. I took a few days to get my bearings – which included finding my way down through a long dark passage called the coal hole to the dining room. The dining room was referred to as the mess deck.

I shared my quarters with three other Wrens. One was an attractive blonde who had been a hairdresser. The other two had worked as a waitress and a dressmaker. Getting to know this jolly medley during our social gatherings was very enlightening indeed. For instance, it was here, for the first time, that I realised the significance of the social divide between dyed-in-the-wool Royal Naval officers (whom we were supposedly trying to emulate), who would wait impatiently for the sun to sink over the yardarm so they could pour their first pink gin with a clear conscience, and the sailors who were expecting a tot of rum. Sadly, neither of these came our way.

Like the rum, food was in short supply. As a result we would eat as quickly as we could in the hope of getting second helpings. We all seemed to be perpetually hungry.

Sharing rooms with all these diverse girls brought to light other discoveries, too: some were wedded to their vests, keeping them on even under their pyjamas when they tucked down for the night. Putting your bra on over your vest then, of course, comes naturally. But there was another rather sensitive problem, to which some people were more allergic than others, which I had first noticed somewhat earlier, when my mother brought a new nanny into the nursery. My recollection of her white shiny satin blouse with mother of pearl buttons remains to this day associated with what used to be called BO – body odour.

I must have been a horrible child, because I immediately pointed out to my mother how the nanny smelled. The vest enthusiasts were rather more prone to this affliction than others. The antidote to this misfortune was described euphemistically as a 'deodorant' and there was a brand called 'MUM'. There was an incredible slogan everywhere at the time, which actually had nothing to do with BO, but which warned us that "Careless Talk Costs Lives"; it was worded "Be like Dad – Keep Mum" – and used to scream at us in whatever form of advertisement we used to read in those days.

Determined to avoid the dreaded BO and having learned that there were very few bathrooms in the buildings, I found myself getting up earlier and earlier to be sure of hot water for a bath.

There were a great many rules to be obeyed at HMS *Pembroke I* and I was often in trouble for breaching them. The nine o'clock curfew was particularly frustrating. One barely had time to go out, and if you did go and found you had cut it rather fine to get back in time, there was no chance of affording a taxi on a Wren's allowance of 10 shillings a week. Sometimes, I ran out of money and couldn't even pay for a bus.

I was in trouble again when I found that a member of the FANY who shared our building was someone I had been at school with. For some mysterious reason we were forbidden to talk to the FANY, but she and I resumed our friendship.

By great good luck she had a powerful motorbike and we used to cheer ourselves up by tearing round Hyde Park on it after lunch – me riding pillion. Though Hyde Park was not as it once had been – by this time there were anti-aircraft guns and sandbags among the flowerbeds – we always felt better afterwards.

Having chosen to become a coder, I discovered that I had to become a writer first and this involved typing and shorthand. I heartily disliked typing, as the letters were covered up so you could not see them and you were supposed to learn them by heart. The only letters I got to know were MR which I thought was Mr. Apparently it meant Margin Release – whatever that was.

Between typing lessons and PT I was invited to do various other jobs which qualified one as a Wren. These including scrubbing the floor and other menial tasks in which I did not excel. There was also squad drill – another torture. This was certainly a diversion from the typewriter, though no female is designed for marching. Vital, to begin with, is knowing left from right. I remember my father telling me about some of our countrymen who were incapable of such distinctions and were made to put straw in one boot and hay in the other, the orders were then given as "hayfoot – strawfoot".

Much worse was later in my career when I had to take a barrack room full of Wrens and drill them myself. I simply could not get the words "About Turn" out at the exact moment when the right foot was correctly poised and thus was in danger of forcing the whole squad to climb up the end wall of the building!

Boarding school had somewhat prepared me for this communal existence, but there were still some surprises. For the first time I was mixing with girls of all classes, whom I would not have met in the course of my rather narrow life. I soon learned that what made people valuable as friends and colleagues had nothing to do with class. Most important was integrity and that was unrelated to social status. I just realised that some people were true to their word and some were not.

Looking back on this broadening of horizons, I also discovered very early on that in living at such close quarters with complete strangers, from every walk of life, the one common denominator which began tentative friendships was a sense of humour; never can this have been more essential. Reflecting on such matters reminds me how harmoniously we all settled down, and how I suspected that my own inadequacies would probably outweigh everybody else's, and that my new comrades would not necessarily agree with me as to what was funny and what was not. Luckily, however, one of the things we were fighting for was a free country.

After a couple of weeks in Kensington, I began to wonder whether I had made a mistake by turning down the job at WRNS HQ. One day on my way to lunch, I met, in the coal hole, the nice officer Nancy Osborne, who had interviewed me. It seemed a fortuitous meeting indeed. I asked her if by any chance the HQ job was still on offer, and before you could say "knife" there I was, safe from Chief Officer Buckmaster.

It was a great piece of good luck for me – and I felt I could start my career all over again, this time under better auspices.

WRENS HQ
LONDON

At the end of February 1940, I took up my new role at HMS *President*, back at the WRNS HQ next to Admiralty Arch. I was still on dry land, of course. HMS *President* was another 'stone frigate'. There were a number of buildings that took the name *President*, followed by a Roman numeral. Together they formed part of the Royal Navy's accounting department.

The HQ job was not thrilling. It consisted mainly of sorting through the applications and references of people who had written in to join the Wrens. By now, the WRNS was considered to be the most fashionable of the women's services. We certainly had the most attractive uniform.

Vera Laughton Mathews had cleverly commissioned fashion designer Edward Molyneux to give the uniform the couture touch. Molyneux was a very successful couturier who delighted high society with his clothes. He dressed many European royals and film stars including Greta Garbo and Vivien Leigh, and would later inspire Balmain and Dior. Whether it was because of the uniform Molyneux created, complete with tricorn hat, or due to the WRNS's excellent reputation earned in the Great War, there was no shortage of applicants.

I quite enjoyed sending the ones I didn't like the sound of to the fate from which I had just escaped! One day I found a letter from my ex-convent school English mistress, trying to sneak in as an officer. I enjoyed wielding a little power over her and put her letter at the bottom of the pile. She did however manage to join the Wrens in the end, creeping in as a direct entry officer.

Our office was next door to where Diana Churchill worked – she was so exactly like her father, the Prime Minister – very animated and obviously extremely entertaining. Peals of laughter were always attracting our attention and she would often come through our office and lighten our day. She never did manage to master her tie, and her collar was always adrift, with the tie floating in vain for anchorage. By comparison, the Chief Staff Officer, Sybil Cholmondeley, the Marchioness of Cholmondeley, who wore her grey hair swept up on her head, always looked as if she had come straight from the hairdresser.

The officers were very kind to the junior Wrens. When I joined, I had no idea there were officers and ratings (ordinary wrens) and was much put out when I discovered that it was only the officers whose uniform included that marvellous tricorn hat!

A rating's uniform consisted of plain navy-blue serge jacket, skirt, white collar and black tie. The white collars were the bane of our lives. They took so much time to put on. Underneath, we wore navy blue knickers which were closed at the knee and known as 'black outs'. We were also supposed to wear stockings made of thick black lisle but often swapped these for stockings made of parachute silk or, later in the war, of nylon.

While the officers' uniforms were bespoke, we ratings were only allowed to go to Hector Powe, a tailor on Regent Street, to have alterations made. There were strict rules about the length of our skirts and poor Mr Powe always faced great difficulties in pleasing his customers while at the same time sticking to the WRNS rules. We were really grateful that we had a uniform which was very becoming, unlike the girls in the WAAF and the ATS, who had to wear shapeless jackets which did them no service at all.

The officers wore hand-tailored navy suits with blue stripes at the wrist to denote their rank. Their hat was the much-admired tricorn felt with the smart naval badge in front. The hat ratings had to wear was a disaster. It was shaped like a melon with a stitched brim and it was very unflattering. We wore it on our heads at whatever angle we thought the best.

Working at the HQ in London I frequently passed our boss, Vera Laughton Mathews herself, who would call me over and remonstrate about my hat, embarrassing me by jamming it down over my ears. I used to feel thankfully responsible for her changing its design as a result of our frequent encounters, and was delighted that the new hat design was based on the sailors' round hat. It was a well-liked choice from its very beginning.

At HQ we usually worked normal office hours with a break for lunch, when we were given a meal ticket worth one shilling and threepence. We mostly went to Lyons Corner House restaurant in the Strand, where you could have quite a reasonable lunch for this small sum. From time to time, it might even include a baked apple with chocolate sauce.

The Corner House was hugely popular and always very busy. There were more than 200 such restaurants across London. The chain had been famous for its smartly dressed waitresses who were nick-named 'Nippies' but a shortage of staff due to the war meant that the Corner Houses were gradually becoming self-service.

Later I discovered that there were marvellous classical concerts in the National Gallery, on the other side of Trafalgar Square to us, and I persuaded those in charge there to accept our meal ticket. They gave us a delicious sandwich and a large cup of coffee in exchange.

The concerts were the brainchild of pianist Myra Hess. When war was declared, she announced that she would not play for the duration of the conflict. Fortunately, she was persuaded otherwise by her friends, many of whom were talented musicians who had fled the Third Reich. Kenneth Clark, the director of the gallery, was only too pleased to host her and her musical friends in his empty rooms.

The National Gallery's most famous old masters had been moved from London to Wales and Gloucestershire over the course of 10 days in the late summer of 1939, when it began to seem inevitable that London would be a target for German bombing raids. However, the galleries were not entirely stripped of art. After a concert, one could go upstairs to see an exhibition of contemporary works by the likes of Eric Gill, Eric Ravilious and Vivian Pitchforth. Later in the war, it was decided that every few weeks one of the exiled pictures would be brought back to London to be displayed as 'painting of the month' to remind us of the gallery's huge importance and raise morale.

The lunchtime concerts were always very busy and we often had to queue to get in. Among the musicians I saw play were Irene

Scharrer and Oda Slobodskaya, a particularly statuesque Russian soprano who set me giggling when she sang *Once I Was a Tiny Blade* – it seemed highly unlikely!

Being based in London also gave me the opportunity to visit my great aunt, Christian Beaton, who was living in great comfort in a Kensington hotel. We called Aunt Christian, after whom I was named, Aunt Tin. She was stepmother to Cecil Beaton, the society photographer, whose portraits were greatly sought-after. He had photographed everyone from Dali to De Gaulle. He would also take some beautiful portraits of serving Wrens later in the war.

Aunt Tin herself was a great character, rarely seen without her dog, a Peke, who had a habit of biting visitors. Whenever I paid her a visit, she would always invite me to stay to dinner and have me recount my adventures for the delight of her friends.

Every Christmas, Aunt Tin would take 40 assorted nieces, nephews and godchildren to the pantomime. Each of us would write a thank you letter and send her a Christmas present, which would remain unopened until the following year when she would return them to us at random. Knowing that we might get it back ensured that we all made an effort to buy something we wouldn't mind receiving 12 months later!

On other occasions, my father would come to take me out to lunch, usually at some rather fusty hotel. Once, I asked him if we might try another venue.

"Where do you want to go? The Ritz?" he responded.

"Yes!" I said, at once.

So we went and it was every bit as grand and wonderful as I had imagined.

By this time my father had retired from the navy and was responsible for the Port of London Authority (the PLA), which governed the Port of London itself, the Thames tideway and the Kent and Essex straits. From the outbreak of war, the PLA had been on alert for a German attack on the buildings and shipping on the Thames. The Royal Navy positioned guard ships at strategic points and barrage balloons were flown above industrial areas to protect warehouses and sheds. Strict security measures were put in place, enforced by the Authority's own police.

The river was a valuable thoroughfare for the city during the Blitz as, unlike the roads, it could never be put out of action by bomb damage. All the same, London's shipping traffic was greatly reduced when the war began, as it was diverted elsewhere in the British Isles to avoid German attack.

Throughout the war, the Thames was heavily targeted and no building seemed more vulnerable than the Port of London Authority's headquarters at 10 Trinity Square, where my father was based. It had a beautiful central rotunda, designed by Sir Edwin Cooper.

Of course, I was concerned for my father's welfare and I rang him up from time to time.

"How are you getting on Pa? Does anyone look after you?" I asked.

In spite of never having even boiled a kettle, and after a lifetime of naval servants pandering to his every whim, he seemed content.

"I have learned how to cook," he told me on one occasion.

"But what do you cook?"

"I cook water and I get out of bed very carefully to save making my bed," he replied.

Sailors are extremely adaptable.

If I had a whole weekend's leave, I would sometimes catch the Friday night sleeper train from King's Cross to Inverness-shire, to see my grandmother. The train was always full and there were occasions when I had to make the whole trip sitting on my luggage in a corridor. The journey usually involved a change of trains in Glasgow and, on one memorable occasion, a change of station too. Worried that I would miss my connection, I accepted a lift from a very kind man in a bakery van. Having made sure that I got to the station in time, he went the extra mile and gave me a rug to keep me warm on my onward passage.

Those weekends spent in Scotland were idyllic, making it hard to imagine the reality of my life in London. In Spean Bridge, the air was fresh and clean. In London, the smog could be horrendous. I remember one occasion, returning from a Scottish weekend, I took a taxi to the Wrenery, as we called our lodgings, only for the smog to be so bad that I had to get out of the taxi and walk in front to guide the driver safely through the roads, while my luggage stayed safe and warm in the car.

One day, I arrived at King's Cross before dawn to find the sky above London lit up as if it were the middle of the day. Only it wasn't daylight. I soon learned that the docks and the East End of London were ablaze.

DUNKIRK

It was now 1940. For the first eight months of the war, the so-called 'phoney war', called the 'Sitzkrieg' by the Germans, nothing much seemed to be happening. At least, not on land. There was plenty of action at sea.

From the very beginning of the war, the German Navy, the Kriegsmarine, posed a great threat to Allied ships. Eight merchant ships had been sunk between September and December 1939 alone. The government knew that because Britain imported so much food, we were especially vulnerable to any disruption of our sea-borne supply lines. Thankfully, going into the war, Britain had the world's biggest navy, with 15 battleships and seven aircraft carriers. They were supported by large numbers of cruisers, destroyers and submarines. The Germans were also disadvantaged by their lack of Atlantic ports. But for how long? In the meantime, food was already strictly rationed. We had very little meat and were allowed just one egg per person per fortnight.

In April 1940, the Germans invaded Denmark as part of their preparations for occupying Norway. Norway was a neutral country at that time, but the Germans knew that it held an important strategic position, providing as it did access to the North Atlantic, the Baltic Sea and the Arctic Ocean. Holding Norway would also protect the German's supply of Swedish iron ore from falling into Allied hands.

British and French troops were despatched to help the Norwegians fight the Germans off. The Royal Navy had some success, but ultimately, the Allies were driven back, distracted by the fighting in France, and Norway fell under German occupation.

After the disastrous Norwegian campaign, Prime Minister Neville Chamberlain lost the confidence of his government and was forced to resign. Thus, on May 10 1940, Winston Churchill became our Prime Minister.

On May 15, the French Prime Minister Paul Reynaud telephoned Churchill to say simply, "We are beaten. We have lost the battle."

Churchill visited Paris and returned with confirmation of the bad news. The French were losing the fight to hold the Germans at bay.

In the 1930s, the French had built a long line of concrete fortifications along their borders with Germany, Luxembourg and Belgium to deter a German invasion. This became known as the Maginot Line, named after the French Minister of War André Maginot. Unfortunately, when the moment came, the Germans sought out the Maginot Line's weak point, on the Belgian border where the fortifications were less concentrated, and were able to march into France from there.

During the six week 'Battle of France', the Germans had driven British, Belgian and French troops to the north of the country, onto the beaches around Dunkirk, where they found themselves stranded with no means of escape. It seemed like a matter of time before the Germans captured the lot of them. Our troops were just 188 miles from home but alas those miles were across the English Channel.

Churchill called the situation a "colossal military disaster', which seemed quite an understatement.

The solution, however, was remarkable.

Vice Admiral Bertram Ramsay and General John Gort of the British Expeditionary Force put into action Operation Dynamo. All along the British coastline, the fishing and sailing communities mustered to the cause. They prepared their boats, some of which were really very small, to make the crossing to France and bring home our soldiers. Together they assembled a rag-tag fleet of more than 800 vessels, which became known as the Little Ships of Dunkirk. They were backed by 39 Royal Navy destroyers, four Canadian destroyers and three French.

Over the course of eight days, more than 330,000 allied troops were evacuated. Some of the little ships made several journeys. The MV *Royal Daffodil*, a passenger vessel, made five trips, bringing home more than 7,000 men. She might have brought more, but on her last sortie, she was attacked by six German aircraft and holed. *Tamzine*, a fishing boat, was the smallest of the Little Ships at just 15 feet long. She can now be found in the Imperial War Museum.

This effort was repeated up and down the south coast. Britain's identity as a sea-faring nation came to the fore with the evacuation of Dunkirk. There's hardly a British fishing town that doesn't have a memorial to that heroic fleet. The British Expeditionary Force lost more than 68,000 troops in the French campaign, not to mention the equipment they had to leave behind. But how much worse might it have been had those Little Ships and their brave crews not made the treacherous journey?

It was in the aftermath of the Dunkirk evacuation that Churchill gave what is probably the most famous of his wartime speeches. Addressing the House of Commons, Churchill said, "Even though large tracts of Europe and many old and famous states have fallen or may fall into the grip of the Gestapo and all the odious apparatus of Nazi rule, we shall not flag or fail. We shall go on to the end. We shall fight in France, we shall fight on the seas and oceans, we shall fight with growing confidence and growing strength in the air, we shall defend our island, whatever the cost may be. We shall fight on the beaches, we shall fight on the landing grounds, we shall fight in the fields and in the streets, we shall fight in the hills; we shall never surrender, and if, which I do not for a moment believe, this island or a large part of it were subjugated and starving, then our Empire beyond the seas, armed and guarded by the British Fleet, would carry on the struggle, until, in God's good time, the New World, with all its power and might, steps forth to the rescue and the liberation of the old."

The speech was not directly broadcast to the nation as many of Churchill's previous speeches had been, but later that same day extracts were read out on the BBC evening news and they made a great impression on all who heard them. I imagined fighting in the hills and doing exactly what he said. We all felt extra patriotic.

Though Churchill reminded us that we should not view what happened at Dunkirk as a great triumph – it was a retreat, after all – he inspired us to new heights of determination that we would not fall to Hitler and his Nazis.

Britain strengthened her resolve.

THE BLITZ

Since the beginning of the war, Britain had been expecting an attack from the air. Air raid precautions such as the blackout, which was designed to limit the Luftwaffe's ability to find its targets, were strictly enforced. At first, such precautions seemed an inconvenience to those of us living in Britain's cities but at last the inevitable happened.

After the surrender of France in June 1940, which had quickly followed the retreat from Dunkirk, Britain was suddenly Germany's last remaining unconquered enemy. And so, Hitler turned his sights on us, mobilising the Luftwaffe to destroy the RAF.

The RAF moved quickly to defend Britain from the airborne threat. One of the first lines of defence they chose was to install special balloons above important military sites and over cities around the country. This was to force the German bombers to a higher altitude so that they couldn't accurately pinpoint their targets.

These balloons, known as barrage balloons, were enormous, described by one of the women who worked with them as being "three times the size of a cricket pitch". They were attached to the ground with heavy cables which no aircraft wished to get tangled up with, and they were painted silver, which must have made them dazzling in the sunlight, adding to the confusion they caused. Furthermore, they were filled with highly flammable hydrogen, guaranteed to explode into a fireball should a bomber try to shoot one down. The balloons were overseen by the RAF Balloon Command and crewed by the Women's Auxiliary Air Force, who winched them into the air from the back of trucks.

The balloons were simple but very effective as a first defence, bringing down dozens of Luftwaffe planes. The planes the balloons did not bring down were forced to fly higher, where they could be more easily picked off and destroyed by the RAF with minimal danger to the civilians below.

Thus, in the summer of 1940, we all found ourselves daily watching what were called dog-fights – battles above our heads, high up in the sky over Trafalgar Square. These fights took place in broad daylight between our gallant Spitfires and the German Messerschmitts. Sometimes a great many planes would be engaged overhead, diving and wheeling as they avoided fire. Gazing up in awe, the crowds would cheer our fighters on.

This Battle of Britain went on for some time until our few, but amazingly brave airmen shot down more Luftwaffe planes than they expected and the Germans suddenly changed their strategy.

Hitler and Göring ordered the bombing of London and Britain's other important cities, with the intention of forcing RAF Fighter Command to engage in what they intended to be a battle that would end in the RAF's absolute destruction.

On September 7 1940, the Luftwaffe began a bombing campaign by night only. This marked the beginning of the Blitz.

The term Blitz is a contraction of the German word 'Blitzkrieg', which means 'lightning war'. This switch from focusing bombing raids on airfields and control centres to civilian targets would turn out to be a grave error on Göring's part. On 15 September the RAF brought down 56 German planes, more than twice the number the RAF lost that same night. It was a shock that would force Hitler to postpone his plans to invade Britain via the south-east coast.

Despite this, the Luftwaffe continued the Blitz for 56 days During that time, London's Underground stations were turned into shelters. As night fell, a significant number of Londoners would pack up their belongings and head down to the platforms, with people bedding down wherever they could. There were even bunkbeds at some of the stations. If you actually wanted to catch a train – they still ran – it could be hard to get through the crowds.

Sometimes the atmosphere was quite jolly, with singing and children playing and parties.

At the Wrenery, on Hampstead Way, Broadhurst Gardens, near Finchley Road, we took our own night-time precautions. We no longer slept in the bedrooms. Instead, we moved down to the semi basement, which had French windows that opened onto the garden. There we slept in double bunks. It was not a comfortable arrangement. The worst of it was that some of my colleagues were terrible snorers who kept the rest of us awake. At the beginning of the night, I would gather up all the slippers I could find to be used as missiles which I aimed at the snorers later on.

We still had to go upstairs to the bathrooms, however. So I soon learned to distinguish between the engine noises of the German planes and our own; a very important distinction to be able to make. At bedtime, I would hurry to finish cleaning my teeth as the sound of brushing made it difficult to hear the shriek of an incoming bomb.

Now that the Luftwaffe, to evade the RAF, had moved to night-time raids only, we were sent home from the office at about four o'clock, to ensure we could get to the Wrenery before dark. Fully ignoring this precaution for our own safety, we quite often used to go to the theatre or cinema on our way home.

Despite the nightly bombardment, London life continued with a semblance of normality. It was the epitome of "Keep Calm and Carry On" (a slogan from a poster which actually wasn't often seen during the war. It has only become popular in recent years). Each morning a new copy of *The Times* appeared on the newsstands. Public transport still ran and, after a brief period at the beginning of the war when they were closed, the theatres had opened again. Some very good shows were put on, including Noël Coward's *Blithe Spirit* at the Piccadilly, starring the highly-talented comic actress Margaret Rutherford as Madame Arcati, a role she would reprise on film in 1945.

I saw *Blithe Spirit*. I also watched the comedienne Joyce Grenfell, niece of Nancy Astor, in a number of highly rated reviews. She would later tour North Africa, southern Italy and the Middle East entertaining the British Troops as part of ENSA, the armed forces entertainments team. The acronym stood for Entertainments National Service Association but ENSA soon became known, somewhat disparagingly, as Every Night Something Awful.

Then there were the Proms, which at that time took place in Queen's Hall in Langham Place, home to the BBC Symphony and the London Philharmonic orchestras. The Queen's Hall was the finest concert hall in pre-war London. Unfortunately, it was hit by a single incendiary bomb on 10 May 1941. The building was completely destroyed, though by some miracle no one was killed. While the concert hall was gone, the public's appetite for music continued. It was in 1941 then, that the Proms, which were still called the Queen's Hall Promenade Concerts, were relocated to the Royal Albert Hall, where they have remained ever since.

Several West End theatres were damaged or destroyed during the Blitz. When the roof of the Queen's Theatre was hit, the upper circle plunged into the dress circle below. The Duke of York's and The Old Vic were closed by bomb damage. The Kingsway Theatre off Drury Lane never recovered.

I was fortunate that none of the performances I attended were ever hit, but I do remember how the whole audience would wince and cringe sideways when the Luftwaffe flew overhead and the explosions got too close. I heard of some audiences finding themselves trapped inside theatres all night and having to sleep in their seats or on the floor between rows when air raids prevented them from leaving the building. I felt lucky to have escaped that.

Sometimes danger came very near, however. During the first week of the Blitz, a bomb fell close by HQ, landing between St Martin-in-the-Fields and South Africa House.

Later, we were travelling in a Number 13 bus which went via Baker Street on our way home to the Wrenery in Hampstead. On the way, we spotted a good film and decided to jump off the bus to see it. After the performance ended we continued home on the same route, and the next morning we were astonished and somewhat shocked to see that where the cinema had been was now a huge hole, taken out by a bomb during the night!

I've recently learned that Madame Tussauds, the famous waxwork museum, was hit in the same attack. I can only imagine how strange it must have been for the ARP wardens to have to search for casualties among the waxworks, which included models of prominent Nazis!

Tragedy came even closer to home one night in late September 1940. Opposite the Wrenery was a row of big Edwardian houses that backed onto a communal garden. One night a stick of bombs fell on our road, demolishing every other house. We were awoken by a terrific blast of evil-smelling cordite, which blew the French windows open into our semi-basement where we were sleeping in double bunks.

We were quite relieved when the all clear sounded the next morning. The Wrenery had escaped the worst, though when I went upstairs to take a bath, the stairs felt very shaky. From the upstairs windows, we could see firemen searching for survivors in the rubble on the other side of the road. Having heard what had happened, Vera Laughton Mathews visited us the next day to see if we were all right.

Over the course of the Blitz, which lasted until May 1941, more than 20,000 Londoners would die. The Blitz touched every part of the city. The rotunda of the Port of London Authority, which my father and his colleagues had hoped to preserve, was destroyed in December 1940. Even Buckingham Palace was hit, with one bomb destroying the chapel. When the King and Queen visited a bomb site in West Ham the following day, the Queen told the people she met there that she felt she could "look the people of the East End in the face" having experienced some of the horror that was being inflicted upon them. The Royal Family's decision not to flee London earned them a great deal of respect from their subjects and restored the popularity of the monarchy.

But it wasn't only London that suffered the Blitz. Throughout the campaign, the Luftwaffe targeted other strategic cities, too. Liverpool and Birmingham suffered enormous damage, as did Southampton, Manchester, Sheffield and Bristol. Portsmouth, Plymouth, Hull and Newcastle upon Tyne were targeted for their ports, as were Belfast, Clydeside and Swansea.

An attack on Coventry on November 14 1940 completely destroyed the city's medieval centre, including the beautiful St Michael's Cathedral, and claimed more than 550 lives. The devastation was so immense, it's said that the Germans rather grimly began to describe bombing a city to rubble as 'coventrating'.

Yet even though I heard the news each day and the Blitz had come so near that night at the Wrenery, it didn't occur to me that I myself could ever be hit by a bomb. With the confidence of youth I never, somehow, felt in any danger.

As a Wren, I could not miss the fact that the war at sea was also intensifying. In September 1940, just as the Blitz was beginning, a German U-boat claimed a terrible prize.

The SS *City of Benares* was a steam passenger ship, built for Ellerman Lines, which had been requisitioned for use as an evacuee ship. Many of Britain's children had already been evacuated from the cities to the countryside in Operation Pied Piper. Now some were being sent further afield, to our allies in Canada. The *City of Benares* was carrying 100 children when it was hit by a torpedo from the German submarine U-48 in the mid-Atlantic. Only 13 of those children survived.

The unthinkable loss of those 87 children caused outrage when it made the news. Arrangements had been made to evacuate more than 200,000 British children to Canada, but any future plan to relocate British children overseas for the duration of the war was now abandoned. The Atlantic crossing was just too risky. Previously, it had been thought that the Germans would not fire on a ship emblazoned with the Red Cross or known to be carrying children. That was clearly not an idea to be trusted. It became more important than ever to win the war at sea.

In the light of the tragic story of the *City of Benares*, in October 1940 Princess Elizabeth, who was only 14 years old at the time, broadcast a message to the children of the Commonwealth on *Children's Hour*, exhorting them to have courage and telling them, "We know, every one of us, that in the end all will be well; for God will care for us and give us victory and peace. And when peace comes, remember it will be for us, the children of today, to make the world of tomorrow a better and happier place."

COALHOUSE FORT

I worked at the Wren HQ for about a year, when I was promoted to Leading Wren and was given a small badge depicting an anchor to sew on my left arm. I was very proud to wear the 'hook' as it was known. I was then appointed in charge of the degaussing range at Coalhouse Fort, East Tilbury, where I would lead a unit of 12 Wrens.

Needless to say, as I left HQ for my new posting, I had no idea what degaussing meant.

Coalhouse Fort was an interesting building, originally one of five fortresses put up by Henry VIII, either side of the Thames, to defend his capital by preventing enemy ships from sailing up the river.

It was at Tilbury that Queen Elizabeth I addressed her troops as they prepared to repel the Spanish Armada, with what has become her most famous and rousing speech, when, dressed all in white and mounted upon a silver gelding, she told her men, "I know I have the body of a weak and feeble woman, but I have the heart and stomach of a King and a King of England too."

The Coalhouse Fort was incorporated into a Victorian coastal defence fort in 1874. It was later modified again to take modern armaments. As the war at sea unfolded in 1939, it once again, occupied an important strategic position.

Arriving at Tilbury, I knew very little about Coalhouse Fort's modern purpose, but I quickly learned the meaning of degaussing.

The gauss, represented by the symbol GS, is a unit of magnetic induction. It is named after the German mathematician Karl Friedrich Gauss, who discovered a means of measuring a magnetic field.

Steel-hulled ships create a magnetic field when they sail and this can be used to their disadvantage. During the First World War, magnetic mines were created that would be triggered by a warship's magnetic field and detonate when she sailed by. Such mines were deployed again in the Second World War. The explosions they caused could result in catastrophic damage to a ship or submarine's hull. Equally importantly, the mere presence of mines could render a sea-lane unusable, hindering the passage of merchant traffic until they were eventually cleared and destroyed. It was of vital importance to keep that merchant traffic moving.

Within a week of the declaration of war, two cargo ships – the SS *Magdapur* and the SS *Goodwood* – had already been claimed by magnetic mines. Minesweepers were sent out to patrol British waters and cut the mines loose from their moorings, so that they would float to the surface and could be safely detonated with rifle fire. Some washed up on British beaches, where they were destroyed by crews who had to be meticulous about not having any metal on their person lest they accidentally trigger. the mines themselves.

The mines were not only used by the Germans, however. In an attempt to keep the Kriegsmarine's U-boats out of the Atlantic, the Allies laid a minefield of their own in the English Channel and later in the North Sea. They were effective, sinking several U-boats, but with so many hazards in the water for offensive and defensive purposes, we had to find a way to protect our navy's vessels.

It turned out it was as simple as preventing the ships from triggering the mines by demagnetising their hulls. Degaussing them.

The magnetic field of a ship could be neutralised by encircling it within a conductor that carries an electric current. In order to do this easily, a degaussing control tower was built between two gun-houses at Coalhouse Fort, while a 'degaussing range' was laid across the Thames.

In naval parlance, the fort was known as HMS *St Clements*. It had been fitted with two 5 ½ inch guns from the ill-fated HMS *Hood*, when that ship's guns were removed and replaced in 1940 prior to its final voyage. It was camouflaged by trees and netting laid over the roof. There was also a radar tower, one of the earliest of its kind, to detect submarines. This was disguised as a water tower. It was marked on the Ordnance Survey map as such.

HMS *St Clements* was manned by Wrens, Sea Scouts and navy personnel. As a ship passed over the degaussing range, its magnetic signature would be checked. A degaussing officer would go out to the ship to take the required measurements, which were communicated to our office by the Sea Scouts using Morse code or semaphore. These were then passed to the scientist responsible for deciding the correct current to be passed through the coils around the ship to render it invisible to the German mines. Any work required was undertaken in Tilbury Docks. Measurements had to be taken as the ship travelled in either direction as any change in the cargo it carried might have an effect.

Though my title was Degaussing Recorder in Charge, fortunately I was not expected to do anything too technical. My task was to direct operations, ordering ships over the range, recording the information required by the scientists and making sure it reached them in a timely manner.

Totally dependent as Britain was on her imports, it was a disaster that we were losing so many merchant ships, not only to submarines in the Atlantic but to these new magnetic mines. Later, all Royal Navy ships had such magnetic neutralising protection built in, but all other ships had to have their vulnerability tested over these ranges and the prescribed wire coils carrying the correct amount of electric current had to be fitted right round the hull.

A LEADING WREN

Although I had no training for anything, except the abortive typing and a little squad drill, as leading Wren I was expected, aged about 20, to be responsible not only for the efficiency and smooth running of the degaussing range and the office, but also for the general welfare of my Wren colleagues.

We were billeted in an old vicarage, under the auspices of the caretaker, Mr Entwhistle, and his wife. Mr Entwhistle was a curious sort of man. He was perpetually grumpy, which might have been due to his suffering from thyroid trouble – he had a very obvious goitre. Whatever the reason, Mr Entwhistle made no secret of resenting having to house us. Perhaps he didn't feel he was being paid enough for his trouble. That certainly seemed to be the case from the way we were fed. On our first morning at the vicarage, we were given porridge. When one of the Wrens dared to say that she did not like porridge, Mr Entwhistle claimed it was actually kedgeree.

There was never enough to eat, to the extent that some mornings before work we would go out and pick mushrooms to supplement our meagre rations, which seemed to consist mostly of sardines and raspberry jam, often on the same plate.

We had to sleep four to a room in camp beds. There was nothing but linoleum on the floor in the bedrooms and as a result we were always extremely cold. This was very bad news for one of my colleagues who suffered from asthma. If she had an attack at night, I would have to sit up with her. I could never persuade her to report sick because she was scared she would be asked to leave. While I could help my fellow Wrens in such practical ways as this, there were some aspects of their welfare that were beyond me.

It is quite astonishing to look back and remember how very ignorant girls of that era were when it came to the facts of life. We had been brought up to believe that 'Nice Girls Didn't' but since no one had bothered to tell us exactly what the things were that we 'didn't' do, all manner of confusion ensued. As a result, many young women lived in fear of accidentally becoming pregnant, which was the worst disgrace that could possibly befall a girl. Could a very smoochy French kiss cause a baby?

At Coalhouse Fort, we were surrounded by a wonderful array of young men: soldiers manning the Fort, sailors and marines of all ranks. We were the only girls in sight! There was only the local pub to sustain this potential social life, so we started our evenings out by drinking with the sailors in the public bar and then progressed on to the saloon bar with the officers. Although we were all longing to fall in love and very susceptible to flattery of every kind, I am glad to say that with all this choice and constant changes in personnel, none of us started any very serious love affairs.

Although I did not find romance, I did make some very good friends during my time at East Tilbury. One of them, Ruth Ashton, remained a great friend until she died just a couple of years ago.

Ruth was a very attractive girl with a fabulous mop of red hair. It wasn't only for her hair that she was much in demand with our sailors. They quickly discovered she was a dab hand at the sewing machine and she was often called upon to alter their square rig uniform, which was already most becoming, so that the trousers were skin tight at the top before flaring out into bell-bottoms that swung in a provocative manner.

Ruth was very adventurous and one day she bought a car from one of the Sea Scouts for £11, soon discovering how to drive it, with very inexpert help from me, recalling what I could from my driving lessons from Willie the chauffeur. Once Ruth had got the hang of it, we went all over the place.

Sadly, one day Ruth's car simply died, so she left it in the Albert Dock and forgot about it until about five years later. By this time she was married to Jimmy Joly, who was also in the navy. She told him where the car had been left and they rushed back to see if it was still there. To their amazement, it was!

Since Jimmy was an engineer by profession he did all sorts of things to it, cleaned it up and sold it for £40. Not a bad deal!

It was while I was at Tilbury that I heard the bad news that another friend, The Hon. June Forbes-Sempill, who had been at school with me at the Assumption Convent, had been killed outright by a German bomb. She died in the early hours of 11 May 1941, the very worst night of the Blitz – a desperate night when every one of our fighters was in the air, giving the enemy everything we had.

German bombers had flown to London on May 10 in a raid carefully planned for the night of the full moon, which they hoped would illuminate their blacked-out targets. The bombing began at 11 o'clock and continued for almost seven hours, with the Germans making more than 500 sorties over the city. The RAF and our anti-aircraft batteries did their best but were able to shoot down only 33 planes. Meanwhile, the Germans dropped more than 700 tonnes of high explosives and more than 2,000 incendiary devices.

The destruction was horrendous. This was the night that the Queen's Hall, home of the Proms, met its end. The House of Commons was also hit. As the House burned, the fire brought down the famous gothic roof of Westminster Hall. Even the Speaker's Chair was lost to the flames. It took 50 fire pumps to contain the blaze. Westminster Abbey, which stood next door, was not spared either. Though it was not struck directly by any bombs, its roof was hit by a number of incendiaries. Parts of the Abbey's roof caved in. Fortunately, most of its treasures had already been moved to the countryside and its stained-glass windows were protected to a degree by having been covered over, but the Deanery was lost.

The loss was not just of buildings, of course. In those seven hours, the Germans claimed the lives of 1,436 Londoners and injured 2,000 more. The blow to London's morale was a hard one.

My friend June was not the sort of person you could ever imagine would be in that sort of danger, protected as she was by her strict and rather grand family, and working in a WVS mobile canteen in Basil Street near Harrods. She was no doubt entertaining her companions with her splendid sense of humour and not paying attention to her possible fate.

She was only 18 and had only just been allowed to do any war work.

THE WAR IN THE ATLANTIC AND BEYOND

It was little consolation that on the very day June died, Hitler's deputy, Rudolf Hess, crash-landed his own plane in Scotland. Hess had been on a secret mission to broker peace. It's not entirely clear whether Hitler had given Hess orders to undertake such a mission – Hess was certainly considered to be a loyal Nazi – but when the crash made it impossible to keep Hess's flying visit to Scotland a secret, Hitler was quick to reassure his allies, such as the Italian leader Mussolini, that Hess did not have the Führer's backing. Needless to say, no peace talks were held. Hess was taken as a prisoner of war and the conflict carried on, not least at sea.

Two weeks later, our navy picked up intelligence that the German battleship *Bismarck*, the largest battleship at sea, and the heavy cruiser *Prinz Eugen* were on their way to the Atlantic to attack Allied convoys. Royal Navy battleships HMS *Hood* and HMS *Prince of Wales* were instructed to intercept them. The skirmish that followed became known as the Battle of the Denmark Strait.

On the night of 24 May 1941, HMS *Hood*, whose old guns were defending Coalhouse Fort, was hit by several German shells.

The damage was catastrophic. *Hood* sank within three minutes and all but three members of her crew were lost. The loss of such an important ship, which had seemed to represent the might of the Royal Navy, had an effect on British morale, especially since HMS *Prince of Wales* had sustained her own damage and had to disengage from the fight, leaving the *Bismarck* to escape.

Bismarck was not to run free for long, however. She was sunk by the British three days later, as she tried to sail back to occupied France for repairs. But it was small compensation for the huge loss of life suffered with HMS *Hood*.

And on June 1 1941, the Luftwaffe were back. This time they bombed Manchester, killing another 70 and injuring 86 more.

Meanwhile, further afield, the Battle of Crete came to its conclusion. Though it resulted in the withdrawal of Allied troops from the island, this battle marked an important turning point in the war: it marked the first time the Allies were able to use intelligence gained from German messages sent in Enigma code.

Of course, we didn't know it at the time, but Alan Turing and his team at Bletchley Park had succeeded in building a machine that could crack the fiendishly difficult and ever-changing code which the Germans used to communicate in the air and on the sea; the Wrens had played a part in this particular success.

It wasn't until the 1970s that the first account of our Second World War Intelligence Information Service was released. Now there are many marvellous and thrilling books written by the brilliant and dedicated men and women who worked in total secrecy, and who can tell us what their brains and foresight achieved in this completely silent battle of skills.

Their accounts show how ill-equipped we were at the outbreak of war, and how, when we did begin to receive and disperse useful information, there was little confidence that it could be relied upon.

We are told how ULTRA was the magic word – the British cover-name from June 1941 for all high-grade signals intelligence, derived not only from Enigma, but from Fish and most hand cyphers. Enigma was the cypher machine used, in various forms, for most signals by the German armed services and several government departments, while Fish was the Bletchley Park cover-name given to German non-Morse traffic enciphered on a machine known at Bletchley Park as 'Tunny' or 'Sturgeon'. Since the need for total secrecy has been relaxed, it is at last possible to explain what an enormous part ULTRA played in our victory, and how many years of war it spared us. The Wrens were involved at several levels, most notably in the 'Y' Service.

The Y Service category was a deadly secret, never described or advertised because of its work for Naval Intelligence, which consisted of listening to intercepts by various means and passing on the (usually coded) messages to Bletchley Park.

Any suitable Wren with linguistic qualifications would be interviewed with this possibility in mind. (Indeed, my sister Anne served as a sergeant in the WAAF in this capacity, listening in to Luftwaffe pilots.) Until the 1970s, the veil of secrecy remained intact, and like so many of the jobs we did, no one who had worked in that department ever discussed it.

When I first began writing about my experiences during the war, back in the early 2000s, I was lucky enough to interview some Y-Service Wrens, who became friends and whose stories I will share here.

SPECIAL DUTIES Y AND Z

SISTER PAMELA HUSSEY MBE

Sister Pamela Hussey MBE, now 97, is a Sister in the Holy Child Order of Nuns in London. In 1939, she was living in the Argentine, but the minute war broke out she prepared to travel to England and join the WRNS. She was already a linguist, but took the trouble to become fluent in Morse code while waiting for a passage. Fortunately, her ship arrived safely, although both the previous ship and the following one were torpedoed and sunk.

Sister Pamela had no guarantee that the Wrens would accept her, as they did not usually take girls from abroad, having such a waiting list of eager volunteers at home, but with her enthusiasm and qualifications she was taken on at once. After some initiation into naval traditions and history, essential naval maxims and slang, such as 'cabin' for bedroom, 'tea-boat' for tea time, 'warming the bell' (being early), or 'them what's keen gets fell in previous' (in other words, the keen ones turn up promptly for squad drill), she was sent off to London to train as a wireless telegraphist special operator, attached to Intelligence.

The training took five months. At the end of December 1942 Pamela passed her qualification and was appointed to the Y station high up on the moors behind Scarborough, an underground construction fiercely guarded by naval police and dogs.

"The Wrens and naval ratings were taken up by transport from their various billets in the town, the short journey being enlivened by singing such classics as *She'll be coming round the mountain when she comes*, *You're my sunshine, my only sunshine*, and *Roll out the barrel*," Pamela told me.

"The wireless room was huge, rows of tables with wireless sets and earphones, naval ratings in one half of the room and Wrens in the other, and in the middle a raised dais on which sat a retired Merchant Navy petty officer connected to the radar stations all over the British Isles and to Station X, as we knew Bletchley Park then. The watches were 7am to 1pm, 1pm to 11pm, and 11pm to 7am, and days off were precious."

Pamela described how the wireless sets she'd been trained to operate worked.

"The sets covered different frequencies, the most important being those listening out for U-boat transmissions. Once settled in your seat, and having taken the earphones from your predecessor (and carefully wiped them on your skirt), one placed one's left hand on the dial and started listening, very often through extremely loud background noise. If in trouble, you called the chargehand of the watch, again a retired Merchant Navy seaman, who would suggest 'Have you twiddled your BFO?'"

The BFO was the Beat Frequency Oscillator, a small dial to the left of the main dial which could be used to explore around the frequency without departing from it. All the time, Pamela was poised with a pencil, ready to take down any signal she came across.

"A U-boat signal was immediately recognisable, and remained unchanged throughout the war: (Dah di di di dah (twice). We called it B bar (the Morse for B being Dah di di di). As soon as one heard this, one called out '500 kcs (or whatever the frequency was) B bar.'"

When any of the Wrens happened upon a U-boat signal, the officer on the dais in the centre of the room would repeat the signal into his microphone so that all the nearby radar stations could get a bearing.

Meanwhile, the wireless operator who had found the signal would scribble it down as it came in. The U-boat messages were very short as they had to surface to send them and they were usually sent in Enigma code, which used letters expressed in the German phonetic alphabet. Once the broadcast ended, the wireless operator would place the paper on top of their set, to be collected by a chargehand and immediately transmitted to Admiralty (if in plain German) or to Station X (Bletchley), where the decoding took place.

The Y-Service Wrens never knew what the messages they had taken down said once decoded. They only heard the German letters. However, Pamela remembered an incident when she was told by the chargehand, "New York wants you to check (a certain group of letters)".

Pamela said that it was "the only time I had any response from 'the powers that be'. On another occasion I had completed a very short signal, probably a U-boat, and the chargehand told me that if I did nothing else for the rest of the war I had already made my contribution to the war effort. Although I was naturally not told why this was so important. Was it because they were expecting a big U-boat attack in the Atlantic, and this gave them the position? Was it because the message itself was important? Was it that fateful message about the *Bismarck*, which gave away her destination?"

Pamela would never find out.

"We knew the work was highly secret. It was enough for us to know that we were engaged in work of vital importance to the war effort, even if it was driving some of us round the bend!"

Very soon after the war ended, Pamela sailed for home in a troopship with other volunteers from Latin America and set about her life's work, tackling poverty and exclusion. She spent many years working among the poor people of El Salvador and earned the MBE in recognition of her work and dedication. In 2018, she was named Chevalier de la Légion d'Honneur by the people of France.

MARY EARL

Because of the hush-hush work in the 'Y' and 'Z' Service, the personnel all had to sign the Official Secrets Act, so very little of their actual activity has ever been described. My friend Mary Earl was one of a number of Wren telegraphists and teleprinter operators at HMS *Flowerdown*, a well-camouflaged Royal Navy radio station near Winchester; staffed mostly by ex-naval signalmen who lived there with their wives. *Flowerdown* mainly concentrated on Italian and German naval communications but also took down German high frequency Morse code.

"There were eight of us who were sent for 'special duties' in a department called Z," Mary explained.

"Our job was 'most secret' and in fact we were the only Wren personnel in the UK in what was at that time an experimental unit. We were an assorted lot. Six, including one Oxford BA, were university types and two of us were very green – virtually straight from school. Rosemary Vaughan (known as Rome) and I became great friends; we were on watch together and shared a cabin. We worked under two scientists, Mr Bainbridge-Bell and Mr Watson

Watt, who together invented the cathode ray tube, which was part of our equipment.

"All the very secret operations took place in a long building with the radio-telegraphists in the first part, the teleprinter operators in the middle and we were at the very far end in a top-secret area (out of bounds to all others). Here there was a great deal of experimental stuff, a room for developing film and a radio set with a ticker-tape machine and a camera in front of a cathode ray tube, manned by a very highly-skilled naval 'sparks'. All the radio operators in the building had to scan the radio frequencies, and when anyone discovered an enemy signal, all the other operators were alerted. Our own operator (one of the older married operators) would rapidly tune in to the signal, switch on the apparatus and we were really 'on the job' – which was to identify the vessel by identifying the set and individual operator specifically by the way he operated his Morse key.

"We eight 'special duty' Wrens worked in four watches – the work was very intensive and when a big episode came up, which usually happened on the eight to midnight watch, we often stayed on with the next watch to help. The *Bismarck* episode saw four of us do a 14-hour stretch! We were identifying individual ships or subs by their radio operators and/or radios.

"Gradually the Admiralty became more interested in the results and would often phone direct, especially 'when something big was on,' and ask for comparisons with other signals. By late 1940, the decoding machines at Bletchley Park were still struggling to break the German cyphers. All their naval transmitters sounded the same, but in our work we began to show a pattern of identification which took on a new meaning. It became extremely helpful to discover that an individual signal had actually been sent by a certain enemy 'sparks' on the same radio set as such and such a signal.

"Our results were sent daily to Bletchley Park by despatch rider to join with all the other enemy cypher messages intercepted by the telegraphists in Y. We felt very proud to think we might have helped to sink the *Bismarck* and 'chase' the *Scharnhorst* and *Gneisenau* up the Channel.

"One day, in a whirl of wavy navy gold braid, Lieutenant Merlin Theodore Minshall RNVR stormed into our unit, all set to take over his new command – us. His first commitment was to set up 70-foot radio masts – we didn't know we could hammer great support staves into the ground with a maul, but we did. Bainbridge-Bell had invented the system and showed us how to use it, but Minshall introduced a new urgency.

"He also improved our working conditions (and believe me they needed it), but he had us running after him like lackeys. 'Hey you there', he said one day, 'you're doing nothing – go and clean my car.' He was a character you'd never forget – one minute infuriatingly rude, and the next a gentleman who would invite us to his elegant home to sit and enjoy classical music with Isolde, his wife. I even used to exercise his bull terrier Clare for him. He had a habit of disappearing for a few days at a time and returning looking a little haggard, and I later discovered about his undercover work in Europe. After the war when the secrecy period was over, he wrote a fascinating account of his adventures called *Guilt Edged*, with the story of his escapades, including his time in Z."

When she had time off, Mary and her friend Rome would sometimes hitchhike to a nearby town. Hitchhiking was perhaps a safer experience during the war than it would be nowadays, but Mary's hitchhiking adventures were not entirely without incident, as she recounted when I interviewed her back in 2007.

"On 12 April 1941, we decided to go to Aylesbury. We kept a note of our various hitches, and on this occasion they included no less a person than our Lieutenant Minshall, after that an American lorry, and then a tar lorry (with a rotten driver), and we had hardly started the next when we saw the despatch rider, Hack, lying by his Triumph 500 motorcycle at the side of the road. The two despatch riders Hack and Wren Hyslop took it in turns to take the urgent secret despatches daily to Bletchley Park. We hastily stopped our driver and leaped out. Hack was out cold, a small crowd had gathered and the local policeman was there. Well! It was absolutely vital that our despatches shouldn't fall into anyone's hands. The nature of our work was such that if the Germans had ever discovered it, they could have stopped us with a simple screwdriver adjustment of their sets each day.

"We were desperate, so we went straight to the spot and grabbed our bag and told the policeman they were our despatches and headed off into the blue. Why the policeman didn't stop us I will never know, but we made a quick getaway and set off, not to Aylesbury, but 80 miles across country to Bletchley Park and with no signposts to show us the way!" Mary revealed.

"I should point out that our pay was very low and we only had five or six shillings each in our pockets. Also, we were very conscious of the conspicuous canvas despatch bag, which was too big to be stuffed inside our uniform jackets or stowed in our service gas masks. Travelling to Bletchley Park was by back roads and in time of war all signposts were removed, so Rome, who had been brought up in Weybridge and had a better knowledge of the lie of the land, laid the trail. We had some very odd lifts – one was a farmer with a rather broken-down vehicle tied together with binder twine, who asked us 'Are you off for the weekend? I bet you've got your pyjamas in there'. 'Of course, and our toothbrushes', I gaily replied.

"With blistered heels – we did a lot of walking – and feeling decidedly weary, we eventually arrived at BP late in the afternoon, and not surprisingly it was very difficult to gain entrance. Our pay books, the despatches etc were taken away and for what seemed a long time we were left in an enormous dining room; we were worn out, very hungry and thirsty, having not dared to stop for more than a couple of scones and a cup of cocoa on the way. Mr Green of the German Naval section turned up with a very welcome cup of tea and told us to take the rest of the weekend off. Sadly, we explained that this would be impossible, as we had to go straight back on duty.

"Eventually we did get the day off and travel vouchers for the return journey, but had to spend the night in a YWCA hostel for 2/6 each! We discovered later that there was a general alert throughout Britain for 'two women dressed as Wrens', who had 'stolen important documents'. However, we had extremely nice letters of commendation from our own commanding officer, Commander Minter, and from the Portsmouth Command Superintendent of Wrens, and later we were given the job of taking some important despatches to the underground premises of the Admiralty, a totally overwhelming experience, which I think may have been a sort of reward."

After the war, Mary moved to New Zealand. She told me how she spent 30 years trying to forget all she had been involved in, in accordance with the Official Secrets Act until…

"Time was up and we could talk about what we'd done and how and why; I was invited to speak to the Royal New Zealand Aeronautical Society and had to spend the next three months desperately trying to remember all the details! Funny old world!"

HOPE MACLEAN

Hope Maclean was another special duties (linguist) Wren, who introduces us to "Freddie's Fairies". Named as such and trained by Freddie Marshall at Greenwich, there were 400 of them.

"I was a fairly early entry into the WRNS (March 1941) and a personal friend of Freddie and Elizabeth Marshall," Hope told me.

"Those who were taught by Freddie at Greenwich had a great respect for him and I feel that later entrants who knew him only as 'Sir' would be glad to know a little more about the beginnings of the 'Fairies'."

Mr L.A. Marshall (nicknamed Freddie) had joined the London Division of the RNVR as an ordinary seaman in 1937. He returned from Denmark, his second home, in August 1939, and because he spoke several languages – including German – he was sent to the Admiralty for intelligence duties. After a brief spell he went to Scarborough, where to begin with the work was routine; but on 16 February 1940 the petty officer of the watch brought him a signal for immediate translation. The message was garbled with some words repeated and some missing, and after deep thought, light dawned on Freddie and he realised it was from one Norwegian shore station to another.

The message read, "Can you take (wireless) traffic from the *Altmark?*" The *Altmark* was on her way from the South Atlantic to the west Coast of Norway, and was carrying many British prisoners from merchant ships which had been sunk by the *Graf Spee*. There was a stream of traffic in German and Norwegian, some of it from the *Altmark's* captain to Berlin in plain language. Freddie learned later that for at least an hour there had been no Norwegian-speaking officer at the Admiralty. As he said, "the ball was at my feet", and he was given immediate promotion from ordinary signalman to signalman.

Hope picks up the story.

"It was discovered that Germans were using VHF – short range intercommunication between vessels, mainly E-boats (German fast attack craft), which would carry out attacks on allied shipping using the convoy routes along the south and east coasts of Britain. For intercept units to pick up these signals, the units would need to be located high up, for example on cliffs with a good view out to sea. Freddie was based at Dover to begin with, but after Admirals Ramsay and Somerville came to inspect, it was decided to employ Wren linguists to assist him with the ever-growing amount of work. Freddie's Fairies began work at South Foreland, then North Foreland and eventually from Peterhead in Scotland and all down the east and south coasts of England to Wales."

The Y-Service Wrens worked in hotels or large houses, and in some places – such as Portsmouth – even in vans. The one in Portsmouth was on Portsdown Hill, high above the town. By now

Freddie had started up the training course at Greenwich where he taught the Wrens nautical German (and nautical English in many cases!), wireless procedures used by the German Navy, and manipulation of the knobs on the sets. The trainees listened through headphones to messages transmitted by Freddie from a nearby control room, and after two weeks, those who had passed the test were enrolled, signed the Official Secrets Act and were kitted up, appointed petty officers and drafted to units.

As the number of intercept units increased, the traffic from them was not only sent to Bletchley Park but also to intelligence centres located next to the operations room in the command bases at Chatham, Portsmouth and Plymouth, where the information was collated. Many of the intercept units had D/F (Direction Finding) towers, linked to them by telephone, in order to obtain a 'fix' on incoming traffic.

Halfway through 1941, Freddie, who had been wearing plain clothes when instructing at Greenwich, was promoted to sub lieutenant RNVR, and by the end of that year, the intercept organisation had grown so large that a mansion in Wimbledon was requisitioned and became the RN Training Establishment, Southmead – with Freddie, now Lieutenant Commander RNVR, as officer in charge. Both Wrens and naval ratings' training courses were transferred there from Greenwich.

Hope Maclean organised a wonderful reunion in London for the Fairies in 2001 but sadly Freddie, who had emigrated to Australia, was not well enough to attend; he sent letters to be read aloud by Hope, and she sent him a list of all those present – everyone had added nostalgic little notes to him; just a month later he died.

JOY HALE AND DAPHNE BAKER

Coincidentally, after learning about the Fairies from Hope Maclean, two more unusual and unexpected stories, with more evidence of Freddie's success, appeared out of the blue, having been buried in the attic of a neighbour.

Joy Hale (Banham) told me, "I was hijacked into Special Duties, when I applied to join the Wrens as a coder. In spite of repeatedly reciting my qualifications in algebra and mathematics, the navy seemed only interested in my knowledge of German, in which I had a distinction at Higher certificate (The equivalent of A-level), and in which I had become fluent while staying with a German family. I was sent to do a German test at the Admiralty, but no one explained why. When my call-up papers came, my category was stated to be Special Duties (L), which meant nothing to me.

"So, on 1 February 1942 I set off to war. Our general training was curtailed because of a shortage of instructors, so I never learnt much about squad drill and missed the lecture on "Sex and Society" which I might have found useful. Twelve of us made our way to Southmead, the training and drafting depot of the Special

Duties category. This was a big Edwardian mansion, complete with ballroom and neglected grounds, situated between Wimbledon and Southfields and commanded by the formidable, (by now), Lt Cdr Freddie Marshall. Both men (mainly Jewish refugees), and women (mostly well-educated daughters of middle-class families) were trained there; the men lived in, and we were billeted in an ordinary family house nearby, where the washing facilities were speculative; I was lucky to meet a lady at Church, who gave me a standing invitation to tea and a bath.

"It was on my arrival at Southmead that I first learned what Special Duties was all about. I was told, 'You listen to German ships talking to each other and write down what they say'. I was somewhat taken aback, as nothing had prepared me for this and I was not confident that I could do it. Moreover, I felt slightly intimidated by the company in which I found myself. I was 18 and straight from a country grammar school, with a strict nonconformist background, and here I was competing with such people as Dawn Thompson, who had just come back from studying singing in the Conservatory at Lisbon, Ann Turner, who had led a sophisticated life in London and several others with confident, bossy manners and far more experience of the world than myself. Only Hilda Frestone seemed to be on a par with me and we became good friends.

"I applied myself to the training and soon discovered if you knew what the ships were likely to be saying, it was easier to hear what they said, and also there was a sort of speechwriting method for writing it all down, so it was not really as daunting as I had feared. At the end of the three-week course Hilda and I found we had passed, whereas Ann Turner and friends had failed and had to do the course again. In the meantime, we were kitted, rated up to acting petty officer and asked which stations we would like to go to.

"I was sent to Coverack where I quickly learned that training is one thing, but real life is quite different. What we had been taught was mainly the sort of radio communications that took place between E-boats on VHF (Very High Frequency), and no mention had been made of monitoring fixed stations on HF (High Frequency). At Coverack we watched the lighthouses on the Brest peninsular, who talked to each other in Q-code and sent their messages in the three-letter Harbour Defence code. This took me completely by surprise, but with the help of the other operators I soon learned to handle it.

"Also while at Coverack I learned the art of D/F (Direction/ Finding), which before radar was the only means of determining where a signal was coming from. Most stations had a specially built separate wooden tower building for this, but at Coverack the apparatus consisted of an H-dipole (a kind of aerial), mounted on the roof and attached to a long pole, which came down into the watch room. The pole was turned by a car steering wheel, with a pointer attached, which gave a reading on a band, divided into 360 degrees and zeroed on north. On detecting your signal, you swung the wheel back and forth until you found the point where the signal faded right out, and that was your reading. If two stations could get a bearing on the same signal, or better still three, you got a fix which could be very useful to our coastal forces."

Having gained considerable experience at St David's near Haverfordwest, and then on the Kent coast, Joy decided to try for promotion to chief petty officer. To do this she had first to learn, by her own efforts, to read Morse at 15 words per minute, and then do a six-week course at Southmead. After some problems in finding people to help her practise, she achieved the required speed.

"So, in January 1943, I went back to Southmead for the course, which I thoroughly enjoyed. In addition to improving our Morse speed still further up to about 25 w.p.m, we also learned the highly disciplined procedures used by the major German naval wireless stations – and the U-boats. It was fascinating stuff. The operators on the big stations sent beautiful Morse and although the U-boats did not often break radio silence, it was quite exciting when one came up.

"At the end of the course those of us who passed were rated chief petty officer. This was a rank of enormous prestige. On the rare occasions when I went into the ports, young sailors would nudge each other, and say, 'Coo, look, a chief sparker!' giving me, no doubt, the same respect accorded to the grizzled old veteran chiefs they had met in the signal schools, and I was not yet 21!

"When the course ended, we were asked where we would like to go. Having been born and brought up in Norfolk, I said 'Anywhere except Norfolk', as I wanted to see more of the world. So they sent me to Sheringham, some 30 miles from my home where I remained for 13 months! I was very happy there and among the girls I met was Biddy Crudys (now Pledge), who has remained a friend for life.

"Sheringham was a small but busy station in the charge of 2/O Elizabeth Marshall, wife of the famous Freddy. The quarters were in a big house on the cliff's edge, and the watch room, half of which was occupied by WAAF intercept operators, stood on Beeston Hump, the highest piece of cliff in the neighbourhood.

There was plenty of E-boat traffic, as both convoy routes passed within visual range. It was here that for the first time I saw the whole intercept operation come together. We picked up E-boat signals and identified the boats; together with Trimingham and Hamsby, where the signals were also audible, we got a fix on them and quickly telephoned the information to the Intelligence Centre in Chatham. Chatham notified Coastal Forces at Lowestoft and Yarmouth, who sent their MTBs (Motor Torpedo Boats) and MGBs (Motor Gun Boats) racing up to the spot. A short time later we heard gunfire, and going out on to the cliffs, we saw the flashes of the 'dust up' going on about four miles out. From the signals which followed, it appeared that the E-boats had been seen off without completing their mission, which had been to place mines along the inner lane. This was a textbook operation, but it was only occasionally that everything worked out so precisely."

Joy had a most varied career, being frequently sent to help out with her valuable qualifications and operational experience. At one time she was very much in the firing line, halfway between Folkestone and Dover, with German guns shelling from time to time. She saw the first V1 doodlebug that came over and blew up in a field further inland.

"After that", she says, "they were a frequent feature in the sky and we would watch our fighters go up and try to tip their wings so that they turned round and went back again.

"After D-Day, and as the Allied advance continued, the German naval stations were over-run one by one, and closed down with such dramatic messages as 'Auf wiedersehen für immer', 'Auf wiedersehen ewigkeit', and even the odd defiant 'Heil Hitler!' We heard Admiral Raeder announce Hitler's death, there was some solemn Wagnerian music and then silence.

"This was the end of the active phase of Special Duties, though not of my naval career. I went on to translate captured German documents at Chelsea, to my OTC at Greenwich, to Germany where I helped to de-Nazify Hamburg, and eventually to civilian life, to the Women's Royal Naval Volunteer (Wireless) Reserve, where I taught Morse to young reservists."

Now comes the second long-lost gem found in my friend's attic which describes what happened to another of Freddie's Fairies.

Daphne Baker (née Humphrys) started the war as a Voluntary Aid Detachment in Canterbury Hospital. Delivered there at 6am by her father's chauffeur-driven car, she spent her days scrubbing and emptying bed pans, until being fetched once more and taken home in time to change for dinner. The promise of being allowed to attend a surgical operation forced her to face the fact that almost any other war work would be preferable.

"Then," Daphne tells us, "I heard that the WRNS were recruiting in Dover and as I'd always hero-worshipped the navy I went straight there, was given a lovely welcome and signed on.

"By the end of September 1939 I was a coder in the Casemates at Dover, working alongside the sailors we were to replace, who gallantly treated us as welcome equals. After a few weeks I was sent, still in civilian clothes, to the second ever OTC course at Greenwich. I was lucky enough to be sent straight back to Casemates as a cypher officer, sharing a tiny dorm in the tiny Wrenery on Marine Parade, with just the road between us and the harbour. I have to say that the phoney war was enormous fun. I loved the work and the friendships and being able to see old friends on leave, and occasionally my parents 10 miles away at Bishopsbourne. Then suddenly there was Dunkirk, and Dover became the focus of the evacuation – the signals piled up so we could only deal with Most Immediate. With difficulty we got permission to work night watches to try to cope. Almost every brass hat in the country was working and sleeping in the Casemates to back up our own Vice-Admiral, Dover, Sir Bertie Ramsay, and we had to pick our way through their sleeping bodies to deliver the signals. The harbour was so crammed with vessels of all sizes that you couldn't have dropped a pebble between them, let alone a bomb.

"If we had time off during the day we used to go down to the quay to meet the troops coming off the boats, and send off letters and messages to their families for them. I think I expected them to be overjoyed to be home, but they walked like automatons, too tired for any emotion. They didn't know then that what looked like defeat would pass into the English language as a refusal to be defeated.

"Among all the losses a nice thing happened. We were on night watch and reports of sinkings were pouring in, including the ship of the husband of a fellow cypher officer. We whisked the signal away so that she couldn't see it, but were heartbroken for her. Early in the morning there was a sudden scuffle and a figure in a blue French smock burst into the cypher office and clasped this girl to his bosom. I don't know how many times he had been sunk and picked up that night, but there was her husband and one happy ending.

"After Dunkirk there were a few halcyon days with the pressure off, and we could swim in the harbour. I must have gone out rather far because on swimming back I realised that troops were laying double rolls of barbed wire along the beach. With a shout of 'Oy, wait for me', I scrambled out of the water and was let through with appropriate jokes from us all about finishing the war on 'the right side'."

Daphne's fate in the Wrens was completely changed one day, when she was languishing in the Wrenery with an ear infection, and the chief officer came in looking worried, and asked if anyone could speak German. Daphne admitted that she could "a bit". She explained that she had spent six months with a charming "German without tears" family in Munich, studying German and music, having one-to-one lessons, but mostly social conversation. She had also done a secretarial course, as her father, who was then ambassador in Baghdad, wanted her to act as his honorary attaché.

She was a natural for Freddie's Fairies, and without further discussion she was sent to the Admiralty, where her interview went:

"Sprechen sie Deutsch?"

"Ja."

"Do you do *The Times* crossword?"

"Yes."

"You're in," they said. And she was.

"My orders," she says, "were to proceed to an empty Trinity House cottage on the South Foreland cliff, (South Foreland is the nearest point in Britain to France, then German-occupied), where I would be joined by two German-speaking chief petty officers and a couple of radio operators from *Flowerdown*, with a van and VHF sets. Our job was to find out whether the German vessels in the Channel were using R/T and if so, establish which frequencies they were using and intercept the signals.

"This was all Top Secret and for even mentioning VHF, now a household word, I could be shot and I still feel guilty saying it. We were also to be out of uniform and our unbelievable cover was that we were factory girls on holiday! Coming back on the train I remember thinking the only way to keep a secret is not letting anyone know there's a secret to keep. (Difficult when you are bubbling with excitement.) I'd been very put off by pompous officers at parties saying, 'Don't ask me what I do,' implying that they were supremely hush hush. I didn't really want to leave my friends and work in Dover, but none of us would ever forget our total willingness to do anything in or out of our power to serve, aroused by Churchill's speeches and leadership after Dunkirk.

"So, within 24 hours there we were on the cliff. The green van, with its tell-tale VHF and DF aerials, and VHF sets was there, parked alongside the three cottages. Freddie Marshall was with us off and on, to explain, encourage and help us. I had only recently discovered that the whole thing was his original idea, and for such a young man to have pushed it through to the top says everything for him.

"The charge-hand from *Flowerdown* and his mate showed us how to work the sets, and which bands we were to cover and search. The first thing we picked up was a flood of plain language R/T (Radio Telephony) from the German Army as it moved through France from village to village towards the coast. The naval transmissions from E-boats or destroyers we were looking for were only expected at night, any movement in the Channel being visible from both sides, so our real job was from dusk to dawn, endlessly sweeping the specified band, pausing on any carrier wave to see if it would turn into a signal, and then on again. I did wonder about this working 12 hours every night, and after about six weeks, went to see my chief officer to ask how long I was supposed to do it. She said, 'For the duration, Humphrys', which seemed at that time a reasonable request, so I saluted and left.

"After a night's work, head buzzing from the earphones, I had to write a report to the Admiralty. My orders were to send this by registered post from the village post office nearly two miles away. We used to walk in, having no transport, and the lady behind the counter would copy out the address, saying 'DSD9 dear? The Admiralty? Is that right?', thus totally blowing our factory girl image. I loved these paradoxes. Just as well, as like many a young officer in charge, I found I was responsible for my crew's welfare, including their pay. To get this, I had to walk to the far side of the village in my cotton dress, with my uniform in a bag, and change behind the hedge, catch the bus into Dover, find the pay office, which was on the far side of the harbour, and then do it all in reverse.

"Our system of communication took a step up from the walk to the post office, when it became the duty of a naval despatch rider to come and collect our daily report. After a long night I had, as usual, translated the signals and tried to make sense of it for the report, when I was told over the telephone that it was too dangerous for the DR to come over, because of the shelling. I looked at our tired drawn faces and thought if the report doesn't go in, it makes nonsense of all our work. So, I got in the van and drove it myself, choosing the narrow coast road as being slightly shorter than the five-mile main road. The chief of staff in Dover Castle took the report and said 'Thank you', without even looking up – so I sleepwalked out again.

"Meanwhile our masters at the Admiralty must have thought we were worth investing in, because we were moved first into the old South Foreland Lighthouse, abandoned because the cliff had fallen away, and then into the windmill about 100 yards behind it. There at last we had a proper watch room, twice as many sets, three times as many CPOs and the van still alongside for D/F bearings. The windows of the windmill faced right across the Channel, and in those early days it was terrible to see our ships being sunk by Stukas, right in front of us. We were stuck to our sets listening on the aircraft frequencies, and I was relieved to see that mine was not the only hand that was shaking as we wrote.

"Another time, we were concentrating on an aircraft, call sign HABICHT, spotting for the German cross-Channel guns, when a shell fell into the sea just below our windmill; the spray came up to the top of the cliff and we heard the spotter say in German, 'Just a bit further and you've got the windmill!' Our scribbling stopped dead and we looked at each other, and I said, 'We had better get under the table', which we did, feeling a bit silly.

"By now the shelling had started in earnest, and for several reasons we came in for a lot of it. Firstly, because a lighthouse and a windmill make a good practice target, even if the Germans did not know we were there. Secondly, if Dover harbour was being bombed, ships would scurry out as close under our cliff as possible, and thirdly, because our own cross-channel guns, Winnie and Pooh, were less than a mile behind us. These were under the command of the Royal Marine Commandos, who became our greatest allies, sending their doctor if any of us was ill, and warning us when they were going to fire, as we had to open all our windows. They also gave wonderful parties for us at their mess in the village and we were heartbroken to hear how many of them never came back from the Dieppe raid.

"Having no diary I can't remember when the Commando doctor insisted on my going on a week's leave – only to discover that I had lost the ability to sleep. You can use willpower to stay awake, but not to go to sleep. It was my only war wound.

"In the summer of 1941 we had an official visit from our much-loved Admiral Sir Bertie Ramsay. After inspecting everything, apparently with favour, he said, 'You know I can't leave you here.' I said, 'But we are very happy, Sir, and would rather be here than anywhere.' He said, 'But what am I going to say to your fathers?' So the station was moved and my new job was back in the Casemates, Dover, to correlate all Y information in the area."

Intermingled with this exciting account of Daphne's war, she told me, "May I say that the whole of my service in Y was irradiated by the fact that I met the love of my life on June 20 1940, the only date I don't need a diary for."

It happened that her home, 10 miles inland from Dover had been taken over by the army, and her mother was allowed to stay on, in part of it. When a friend wrote to her mother asking her to be kind to her gunner son, she wrote back, "I can't be kind to anyone. I'm occupied. But I have a daughter in Dover. Tell him to ring her up.

So Alfred Baker and I met on a blind date at the two-mile limit from South Foreland. A few days later coming off watch, I saw the eastern arm at Dover – where he was stationed – being systematically dive-bombed, and shed a tear. But he survived and from then on, we spent every rare moment off duty together.

"And in August 1941, after leaving South Foreland for the last time to go on leave, my sadness was forgotten in getting engaged to Alfred."

BLETCHLEY PARK

As well as Y and Z units in the Naval Intelligence Service, there was Bletchley Park, or Station X, itself – always surrounded by a mysterious and impressive aura – and where a large number of Wrens worked alongside civilians.

The Wrens played a valuable part in at least one particular aspect of this organisation. Alan Turing, the especially brilliant mathematician, had constructed a mechanical precursor of the modern electronic computer to speed up the mathematical calculations performed by the crypto analysts, and some 1,200 Wrens were employed to tend the machines. It was monotonous work, which wasn't relieved by any real kind of social life because of the strict security accorded to the role. The Bletchley Wrens had to content themselves with the occasional message of recognition from the Prime Minister, who commented "the Chickens were laying so well without clucking".

Jane Fawcett MBE Hon FRIBA FSA gives us a splendid overall description of what working in 'the engine room' at Bletchley Park was actually like.

"Before joining Bletchley in February 1940 at the age of 19, I trained as a ballet dancer at Sadler's Wells under Ninette de Valois. This was an incredibly exciting period when the company was being formed; new ballets were appearing almost weekly and Frederick Ashton, Margot Fonteyn and Robert Helpman were emerging as great artists. We were taught by the famous Russian coach (Nicholas) Sergeyev and by the great Ninette herself.

"However, when the war began and many of my friends were called up, I decided to do a secretarial course in preparation for doing something useful. Soon after, two of my friends wrote from Bletchley to say they were seriously short of staff, that the work was important and encouraged me to join them. At about this time the German operational code, known as Enigma, had been cracked by the Bletchley codebreakers, and everything was taking off.

"I was invited to go for an interview with Stuart Milner-Barry, a brilliant mathematician from Cambridge and the head of Hut 6. As there could be no advertising for staff, recruitment was done on a very personal level, and was even rather furtive and secretive. Milner-Barry was very shy and had no idea how to conduct an interview, but he did find out that I had learned some German (on a three-month visit to Switzerland, just before the war), that I had done a secretarial course and that I had several friends already working at Bletchley. So he offered me a job – at a miserable salary – and took me to see the boss Commander Denniston, who firmly explained that the work being carried out there was extremely important and highly secret, and that I had to sign the Official Secrets Act and never say anything about it – and I never have.

"I was put into Hut 6, which was where the German Army operational code messages were decoded, processed, translated and distributed. I was very lucky to be there.

"The hut consisted of the Preliminary Room in which incoming messages were received and processed. Next came the Registration Room, largely staffed by clever female graduates, known as the Blisters, many from Newnham College, Cambridge, where Milner-Barry's sister was Vice-Principal; then the Codebreakers Room where the most brilliant mathematicians worked. Had they not broken the Enigma code it is quite possible that we would not have won the war.

"When they had broken the code for that day, they passed on the messages with the new settings to us in the Machine Room – working the Enigma machines. We had to decipher the coded messages and turn them into German. When I first arrived, there were only about nine of us acting as a link – unknown to the Germans – between German High Command and Whitehall. We worked three eight-hour shifts, and often in times of crisis we worked 16 hours, or even occasionally for 24 hours at a time. Sleep seemed fairly irrelevant. Sometimes after a night shift I would catch the train up to London and meet Teddy (later her husband); we used to go to HMV and shut ourselves in and listen to Mozart and fall in love – then return in the evening to work the night shift again.

"When we had typed up and decoded the messages into German, some of which came directly from the German High Command, we handed them on to Hut 3 where the linguists lived; they had to translate them and determine the subject matter and decide which department in Whitehall to send them to. Some of the most urgent operational messages went directly to Churchill, to whom we had a direct line, both by telephone and teleprinter."

Jane pointed out how Bletchley grew from 200 staff when she joined in 1940 to about 7,000 when she left, many of them members of the WRNS, WAAF and ATS. "Secrecy was instilled into all of us and the Germans never discovered what we were doing. It has been estimated that our work, and the fact that it was never revealed, shortened the war by two years or more and of course saved thousands of lives.

"In September 1941, Churchill paid us a secret visit to thank us for our contribution to the war effort, and said 'You are the geese that laid the golden eggs and never cackled'. His visit gave us all a big boost and an incentive to work even harder.

"Shortly before this, Milner-Barry and other senior staff members decided to write a letter to Churchill complaining about the under-staffing, poor accommodation and under-equipment, all unacceptable considering the importance and urgency of our work. When Milner-Barry arrived at Number 10 and asked to see Churchill, he was asked who he was and what he wanted; unable to explain because of the Official Secrets Act, he had to leave the letter in his Private Secretary's hands, who promised to deliver it personally."

Jane explained to me that Churchill immediately issued one of his famous directives to General Ismay, Chief of General Staff, saying "Make sure that they have all they want. Report to me that this has been done. Extreme priority." Across it in his own hand he wrote, "Action this day". Things improved from that moment on.

Jane continued, "Up to this point I must tell you what conditions were like. We worked in large sheds, mostly without heating, though there were one or two coke boilers which smoked, so we had to open the windows to let out the smoke. The sheds had no insulation, concrete floors, windows covered in blackout material, trestle tables, collapsible chairs and unshaded light bulbs. They were hot in summer and very cold in winter when we worked in coats and mittens.

"At night we had to fight our way in darkness, round the lake, through trees and bushes to the canteen in the big house, and through all this again to find our minibuses to take us home. My first billet was in a council house in Bletchley with a friendly young family. He was a driver for the London Brick Company under whose chimneys we lived; the acrid smell of brick smoke has remained with me ever since. The family had two small boys, both lively and noisy and not compatible with my need to sleep during the day. Eventually I was saved by some friends of my father, the Bonsor family, who lived in a magnificent neo-Elizabethan house, Liscombe Park near Leighton Buzzard. They invited me to bring one or two friends to live in their staff wing, which was then empty. This was a great improvement on the council house and we were very grateful; but we still had the noise problem, as we were sleeping over the back door where all deliveries were made, wheelbarrows full of vegetables and the gardeners thumping their boots and banging the door. We also had a long walk in pitch-black night to the pick-up point for the minibus to take us to and from work; the whole countryside within a radius of 20 miles was serviced by a network of coaches and minibuses creeping along the lanes in the darkness.

"Some of the men were billeted in pubs and probably had more fun than we did. There was the Duncan Arms in Great

Brickhill, which became known as the 'Drunken Arms', where some of our more spirited colleagues lived.

"When we did have some leave I used my little motor bicycle, 'The Famous James', to get from Bletchley to Ugley in Essex where my family were living. This was a cross country journey through cornfields, and in the summer it was rather beautiful. However, the two-stroke engine was not designed for long journeys, and when the plugs heated up the engine stopped and I spent many hours sitting in a ditch while it cooled.

"Because of the strict security we lived in a very tight community, a closed society where we made our own entertainments. We had a number of societies, which we founded and ran and to which most of us belonged. One of my favourites was the Scottish Dance Society run by an enthusiastic eccentric from Cambridge called Hugh Fosse. He dressed up for the part with a kilt and Scottish brogues, laced up over his calves. He was very tall and thin and pranced about demonstrating the dances with considerable spirit. As a dancer I thought he was wonderful. Then there was the Choral Society and the Drama Club, which put on plays and pantomimes – all good fun.

"Rounders was also spirited but, as we had no posts, we had to use the trees round the front of the house as markers, which caused much merriment and arguments as to whether a player had reached the spruce or been caught out as he left the oak.

"In spite of these diversions, our lives were much overshadowed by the knowledge that the faster we worked the more lives we might save, and the tension this produced affected us all, from the cryptographers and the girls in the Machine Room to the girls hammering out the messages and producing sense out of chaotic rubbish; from the translators turning cryptic messages into comprehensible language to those despatching them to the correct recipients; we were all on a knife edge, aware of the horrors threatening our very existence.

"There had been a period when we had great difficulty in persuading the Admiralty that what we were telling them was really true, because it seemed so improbable that we should know in advance exactly what the Germans were going to do. When we told them that the *Scharnhorst* and the *Gneisenau* were coming out of the Baltic to attack our fleet in the North Sea, the Admiralty failed to believe us, and HMS *Glorious*, one of our vital aircraft carriers, and two destroyers, were sunk, with the loss of 1,500 men. We felt very bitter about that.

"The most thrilling night was the sinking of the *Bismarck*. She and the *Prinz Eugen* had come out to attack our shipping, sinking HMS *Hood* and badly damaging HMS *Prince of Wales*, and had then escaped and disappeared. I was on duty all that night and the next day, while we frantically tried to find out where she was going, so we could prevent her reaching safety in harbour. We picked up a message from the Luftwaffe's Chief of Staff, worried about his son, who was serving in the *Bismarck*, asking where she was going. We intercepted the reply saying she was going to Brest. This time the Admiralty did believe us and she was attacked and sunk.

"During the Blitz, we received the strategic orders from the Luftwaffe and were the first to intercept all their tactical orders on where and when to attack. This was one of our darkest hours when the Germans were carrying out systematic bombing attacks on many of our historic towns. We were crucially short of anti-aircraft guns, so, if we were able to transmit the information about where the next attack was going to take place by lunchtime, it enabled Whitehall to order the transfer of the anti-aircraft equipment from say, Coventry, which had been attacked the previous night, to Plymouth, which was planned for the following night. This might mitigate the force of the attack.

"In July 1941 we at last managed to break the naval Enigma code which carried information on all U-boat movements in the Atlantic. This saved one and a half million tons of shipping, thwarting the Germans' attempt to starve us to death, which at this time they were near to achieving.

"In 1943 during the North African campaign we received advance warning of the movements of Rommel's supply convoys, on their way from Italy with reinforcements, allowing the RAF to sink many of them. We also informed Montgomery in advance about Rommel's movements in the field, enabling him to plan counter attacks. This was crucial to the defeat of the Africa Corps, which was a turning point in the war.

"When it came to D-Day, Bletchley was much involved in deceiving the Germans about our invasion plans; as a result Rommel ordered two divisions to proceed from the Normandy beaches to the Pas de Calais region, enabling us to get our foothold during the vital first three days, while he struggled to return them to Normandy. A signal from Bletchley also diverted one of our airborne divisions from landing among the German troops.

"After VE Day I was released and started my training to become a singer at the Royal Academy of Music. But, before leaving I was interviewed by Commander Travis and asked to sign the Official Secrets Act again. His last words were: 'I cannot stress too highly the necessity for the maintenance of security; it is as vital as ever not to relax from the high standards of security that we have hitherto maintained. The temptation now to own up to our friends and families as to what our work has been is a very real one. It must be resisted absolutely.' And it was. End of story."

Another young girl, who had worked at Bletchley on 'low-level' Luftwaffe codes and cyphers, felt that for some of the young people there, it was quite literally the time of their lives.

"I'm terribly grateful for the five years I had there. It was something quite out of this world. It was a very broadening experience, because of all these extraordinary people gathered together; many of us had come straight from school and were lifted up immediately into an atmosphere that perhaps we would never have experienced. Or that would only have come to us very, very slowly in our different lives. To be with people for whom books, music, art, history, everything like that, was a daily part of their lives, it was an absolute blossoming for me, and I have to say that, though I have had many wonderful friends since, I've never again experienced that atmosphere of happiness, of enjoyment of everything that meant life to me."

It is rather touching to read how so many young Wrens made their greatest permanent friends, at that time, when they needed them most – after leaving home, often for the first time, and being plunged into communal life with complete strangers – finally sticking to each other all the 60 years since their Wren service. It is not easy, even now, to forget the mixed excitement and anguish of starting life in a new establishment. Would one be lucky enough to find a kindred spirit? We took our jobs extremely seriously and gladly endured considerable hardships, knowing that the men we were replacing were probably in much worse straits.

THE END OF MR ENTWHISTLE

Back at Coalhouse Fort, our landlord Mr Entwhistle came to a sad end in the summer of 1941. The story of his demise is rather grisly. In our flippant and heartless manner and after yet another ghastly meal, we often used to say, "I do hope one day someone will come and take him away and cut his throat," referring to his goitre.

Imagine my shock and horror when on my 21st birthday somebody did exactly that, and my birthday treat was an invitation to view the poor man's remains in his coffin, returned to his home after an operation to remove his goitre proved fatal, and where his lying-in-state took place on the dining room table. I remember trying tactfully to duck out of this by saying, "No really, I would rather think of him as he was…"

The day had begun rather dramatically at work, when I was called to the telephone by the hospital, and asked to tell Mrs Entwistle that her husband had died during the operation and would I please inform her. There was of course no telephone at the vicarage. I remember putting on my uniform hat, which somehow seemed necessary for the sombre occasion, and walking up to the vicarage; I then persuaded her to sit down in her parlour where I broke the dreadful news, which to my relief did not seem to displease her terribly.

This, however, was still my 21st birthday. By the time the sun was over the yardarm, several cheerful friends, Philip, Peter and Jerry, and our degaussing sailors, rolled up with bottles of this and that and before long we had this party going.

Unfortunately it was a rather small room for such a party, and apart from the macabrely occupied dining room table, there was nowhere much to put things.

Mrs E was just having her third gin and getting rather tearful, when Jerry, after raising his glass and proposing a toast to "Up spirits!" became intoxicated by his own wit, howled with laughter, and absentmindedly put his glass down on the coffin. This caused the whole party to disintegrate into uncontrollable giggles, where-upon Mrs E, overcome with such a heady mixture of emotions and no longer able to assimilate what was going on, sank silently to the floor. Thus I have never been able to forget my coming of age.

One day quite recently, I was invited back to Coalhouse Fort. They intended to make a museum out of the old fort and thought I might have something to contribute to this venture. I was delighted to go back and hoped to be able to have some memories to furnish them with. To my disappointment there was nothing I could recognise or remember – even the fort seemed a different shape. Where was the old vicarage we lived in? Where was our office and the place from where the Sea Scouts sent messages? I felt there should be something left – even after 80 years.

AN OFFICER IN TRAINING

After a year dedicated to degaussing, it was suggested that I go before the Officer Selection Board. To my great pleasure, I was promoted and sent to attend the Officer Training Course at Greenwich.

Having lived in that shabby vicarage under the auspices of Mr Entwhistle for quite long enough, I was delighted to be getting away, but I could not have anticipated quite how dramatically my lodging circumstances would change.

I arrived in Greenwich by ferry, disembarking at the pier once used by Elizabeth I and her great explorers Sir Francis Drake and Sir Walter Raleigh. It was a suitably historic start to my new adventure, which would be taking place at Greenwich Palace itself.

The Palace stood on the site of the Palace of Placentia, built by Humphrey, Duke of Gloucester, in 1443. It was rebuilt by Henry VII, who used it as his home. Henry VIII was born there, as were his daughters, the future queens Mary I and Elizabeth I. However, Placentia was allowed to fall into disrepair during the English Civil War, when it was used as a prisoner of war camp. Afterwards,

Charles II planned to rebuild the palace, but his commission was never completed. It was King William III who decreed that the site of the palace should be used to build a charitable institution for naval veterans. The architect he commissioned to design the buildings was Sir Christopher Wren, who was already notable for his work at Hampton Court Palace.

Wren wanted the Royal Hospital for Seamen, as it was then called, to embody Britain's importance as the world's most powerful maritime nation. Thus, ably assisted by Nicholas Hawksmoor, he designed and built a complex of baroque buildings on a magnificent scale. The results were breath-taking and these were the buildings in which I would be doing my officer training.

The lectures and lessons we had were interesting enough but having all our meals in the Painted Hall was the utmost luxury. The room in which Lord Nelson once lay in state was now the Naval College's dining room.

Even at breakfast, we were waited on by Wren stewards, who served us delicious coffee in big white china cups decorated with the blue stamp of the Admiralty. One of the most important parts of officer training related to cultivating a lady-like manner. A Wren officer should not be caught eating peas off her knife. We were aided in this endeavour by the senior Wren officers and the Hall itself, which encouraged a refined atmosphere and polite conversation. One could not be too rowdy when gazing in awe at Sir James Thornhill's early 18th-century trompe l'oeil paintings, made more beautiful by candlelight. Thornhill's murals, which took 19 years to complete, earned the Painted Hall the title of 'Britain's Sistine Chapel', and earned the artist his knighthood.

My friend Mary Wynn Jones, who worked at the College as one of those expert Wren stewards, told me how she came to love those marvellous paintings. She wrote to me many years later, saying that she would walk into the Painted Hall, "always with a feeling of pride and privilege, never ceasing to find pleasure in the richly coloured paintings…" She also told me that, "to study the latter in some quiet off-duty hour, we Wrens would lie on the tables, guidebook in hand, trying to identify the separate pictures."

The wonderful Palace was such a contrast to the squalid living quarters we had endured at East Tilbury, though there were moments when it didn't feel like such a luxurious billet. I was there in the late autumn and it was extremely cold. In such conditions, rushing along the stone passages in a skimpy dressing gown looking for a bathroom was something of an ordeal, particularly since it wasn't always easy to find one's way as one corridor looked more or less like another.

Mary Wynn Jones had some wonderful stories about working at Greenwich. When I told her that I wanted to write a book about Wrens during the Second World War, she was only too happy to lend me her experiences, which give a vivid picture of daily life at the Naval College, both for those who worked there and those, like me, who were passing through.

"I survived the back-breaking task of swabbing the dusty flag-stoned floors of the lower regions of the College with a long-handled mop at the crack of cold, dark dawns, and graduated to the pleasanter tasks of bed-making for the junior officers, where my nanny-training stood me in good stead, and thus to the cleaning of 'cabins'. No luxury of vacuum-cleaner nor even the more modest carpet sweeper in this austere establishment – instead I learned to clean carpets by the almost archaic method of first sprinkling them liberally with wet tea leaves, which were then brushed up plus the dust so collected by them, by vigorous use of a hard-bristled broom, smaller mats being taken 'below', to be either shaken or beaten depending on their size, outside. Then down on hands and knees to apply wax-polish to the wood or lino surrounds, ditto to buff to a shine. Except where there was sufficient floor space to be able to tie dusters to the feet and slide energetically over the surface – most effective and great fun, especially swishing and swooshing down the long corridors. Turn and turn about, I and my colleagues had the unenviable task of scrubbing the wide cold stone stairs leading from one floor to another… all of which provided excellent exercise, though there was not a great deal of fun to be had from having afterwards to wash out wax-polish-impregnated dusters and rough floorcloths with nothing more than hard yellow soap and hot water in horridly chilly, ancient stone sinks.

"Finally, I was introduced via the Wren Officers' Mess in Queen Anne's block of the College, presided over by the so-elegant and delightful Miss French, (Superintendent WRNS in charge) to the niceties of waiting at table. 'Menu and food from the left, drinks from the right, anticipate needs' was her mantra. I learned quickly, seeming to have a natural instinct for it, with the advantage of coming from a good middle-class home with properly set table, and parents who taught their children to respect it… Here I was happy to stay, once I had recovered from the sheer terror of my first day, when, neat in my mess uniform of princess-line white coat, its blue mandarin collar opening over knotted black tie under fresh white shirt collar, and with pristine white gloves to protect my hands from hot plates, I saw each side of the long tables to which I had been allotted in the Top Hall, filled with some 50 identical faces atop identical naval uniforms. And was panic stricken. 'But,' I exclaimed in horror, 'I shall never be able to sort them out – they all look alike.' 'You will – they may look alike, but believe me, they are not', confidently assured Miss French, my guide and guardian angel of those first mazed days. I looked at her sceptically, and yet during those days, watching the smilingly confident ease with which this slim young girl darted about her duties, I slowly began to see a little light.

'"Damn it all, you're not a moron,' I told myself and firmly set myself to the task of mastering the intricacies of waitressing, carefully noting any particular feature of my 'charges' as they gave their orders – the red hair for coffee, the wide smile for tea, and a glass of water for that dishy blond American, plus strawberry jam with his breakfast kipper! Beyond that and concentrating on placing the right order in front of the right person, and where I had to go for which order, I could spare not a thought; going to bed at night with legs aching and feet sore from the hard stone floors, my head awhirl with spinning tea cups, cascading plates and the mind-numbing fear of spilling a plate of soup over one of those elegant doeskin uniforms. Yet at the end of a month or so, I delightedly found that the computer in my brain was clicking over with a smooth efficiency, and that not only could I confidently fan out several soup dishes and plates, or cups and saucers between my fingers and up my forearms as I sped up and down the Long Hall, but that I could do it whilst exchanging light-hearted banter with these suddenly endearing youngsters, thoroughly enjoying the business of the job, and priding myself on giving neat efficient service.

"Hectic days they were, with only a handful of staff to deal with the seemingly endless stream of young officers who came swarming in for their meals which had to be in two sittings for each meal. Concurrently with this, the other half of my duties lay in looking after the 'cabins' of three or four senior naval officers and the valeting of their persons, the majority of whom had been called back from retirement in order to release younger men to active service. This personal-sounding service turned out to be no more alarming than waking them at 7am with a cup of tea, taking their suits out to brush and their shoes to clean while they drank it, returning with a jug of hot water for shaving (no running H & C, but good old-fashioned basin and ewer, and I regret to say, also chamber pots under the beds.) I would then carefully drape the back of a chair with their clothes in the correct order for donning, shoes neatly to attention underneath it, and after giving them a final time check, leave them to it. At first I had been a little apprehensive about all of this, but I need not have been. These august-sounding men, all 'pukka' RN captains and commanders, were only older fathers and grandfathers in uniform and I very soon developed an easy friendly rapport with them. I also rather suspected that they quite liked a smiling young girl to wake them in the mornings.

"Cabins were cleaned between serving of breakfast and the attendance at 'Divisions', (the naval version of school assembly) and lunch. The afternoons were given to drill lessons under a Royal Marine sergeant, which greatly pleased my sense of order and love of physical movement; to any necessary pressing of suits, well instructed by a naval PO; the odd hour or so for personal pursuits and to the setting out of tea things in the various ward rooms for the officers to help themselves, the latter duty depending on whether I was on or off watch. In the evenings there were the cabin black out curtains to be drawn, beds to be turned down, pyjamas laid out and carafes to be filled with fresh water before going down to the Hall to lay up for and serve at 7.30 dinner."

Such were Mary's busy days and all the time, the Luftwaffe continued its bombing campaign. Of course, the enemy planes followed the course of the Thames on their way into London and thus Greenwich and the College was right on their flight path.

When the air raid warnings sounded, we retreated to the 'catacombs'. In these enormous vaults, Sir Christopher Wren had unwittingly designed the perfect bomb shelters. Naturally, we Wrens were separated from the male naval personnel for the sake of propriety. The catacombs were not terribly comfortable – one often had to share a triple bunk – but they were very safe.

Mary takes up the story, telling how during her time at the College, she too sheltered down in the catacombs until, "we moved a little higher up under the billiard tables in the games rooms, and finally fed up with never having a proper bed to sleep on, in our own bunks above in the Wren quarters in King Charles' block and below the constant explosion of bombs, zooming of aeroplanes and crack of gunfire in the skies above. This was the accompaniment to the dances in the Gunroom where one officer, Captain Johnny Doyle, forever requested his favourite Glenn Miller record – *In the Mood* – which was still resonating loudly over the shocking news of the loss of the *Prince of Wales* and the *Repulse* that rippled round the dance floor on that terrible night in December, bringing us all to a sudden and shaken standstill. All those young lives snatched away, some of whom we had laughed, joked and flirted with only weeks before. 'Twas so difficult for mind and heart to encompass, and all we could do was to pay them our loving tribute of our silence and our tears.

"This was also the time of the incendiary bombs. Little bombs that burst into flames on impact, many of them landing on the roof of the College buildings. The young officers were often kept busy at night dousing with fire hoses. Indeed it was from one such night that my current 'date' came rushing in for breakfast, excitedly waving and shouting, 'It's all right Mary – I've saved the tickets!' His quarters were awash, many of his possessions had been burned, he was blearily red-eyed, with smoke-smeared face and uniform – but the tickets for *Gone with the Wind*, then on its first London run at the Odeon Leicester Square, were safe! Dear Philip M – how I bless him over the years for that. I had read and fallen in love with the book when it first came out and it has been a lifelong companion to me ever since.

"At night, as the bombs whistled around, and in answer to a hurried whisper at table of 'Meet me at the West Gate at 8', or a pencilled note passed in the saucer of a cup, we Wrens would cheerfully ignore an 'Alert' to dash through the flak-ridden streets, when the day's duties were over, for a visit to the cinema, a meal in the West End, to some dance-hall there or at some other service unit, or in the College itself. For youth calls to youth and I came to love the rush of these fresh-faced, hungry young men as they came streaming in for their meals, gleefully freed from their classes, high spirits at last uncontained; it never ceased to give me astonished delight to have my presence greeted with a joyful – 'Here she is! Come on Smiler. We're waiting for you!'

"Thinking about it at times, I supposed mine was not a very glamorous role to play in the war. But I did not mind. I was neither vain nor ambitious, and was quite content to give of my best as an unglorified waitress-cum-housemaid. Somebody had to do it, it freed a man for active service and, unsure as always of other capabilities I might have, I knew that this at least I could do. More than that, it fulfilled some deep need within me to give of myself (a leitmotif, as I later discovered, that ran through all that I have subsequently done) and with my usual zealousness sought to do it as well as I was able."

The service of Mary and her Wren colleagues at the College was invaluable. Some 8,000 Wren officers were safely trained at the College during the war and they all benefitted from the impeccable care of Mary and her fellow stewards.

During my own time at Greenwich, we were visited by Princess Marina, the Duchess of Kent. The young duchess, who was a princess of the Greek royal house before she married Prince George, fourth son of George V, was widely considered to be one of the most beautiful and glamorous women of the time. During the war she was Commandant of the Wrens and I was part of the guard of honour for her inspection.

I spent just a couple of weeks at Greenwich before, having passed the Officer's Course, I was made to do the cypher course because I had originally volunteered to become a coder.

I had long since discovered that code and cypher work was nowhere near as glamorous as it sounded so I tried to persuade my superiors that I wanted to become a plotter instead (I had decided that plotting was much more interesting). I had no luck. They insisted I do the coding course anyway.

It was at this point that the Admiralty Jokes Department, as I called it, stepped in, ordering me to report to Mount Wise Headquarters in Plymouth as a plotting officer. I was delighted to have escaped a career in coding! As a plotter I would be entitled to read all those laboriously decoded messages anyway and also have complete access to secret documents, such as the 'Pink List', which was especially valuable as it listed the whereabouts of all the ships in the navy. You could thus discover where your latest young man was likely to be!

Now, as a third officer WRNS and with my tricorn hat at last, I felt very happy but also a little nervous of whether I would be capable of plotting – not having the faintest idea about it.

As seemed to be the case throughout my WRNS career so far, all I could do was cross my fingers and hope for the best!

PLYMOUTH

In late February 1942, I left London for Plymouth by train, on Isambard Kingdom Brunel's Great Western Railway. It was an extremely pleasurable journey, passing through beautiful country-side all the way. For a while after Exeter the trainline hugged the coastline so closely you felt you were almost on the beach. I came to learn, as I made the journey on several occasions that spring, that sometimes the waves would wash right over the tracks.

At the other end of the journey, however, the view was not so appealing. As we have seen, London was not the only British city to have suffered the Blitz. Plymouth had seen more than its fair share of bombing raids. It was a prime target for the Luftwaffe because of the dockyards at HMNB *Devonport*, where Royal Navy ships and submarines were brought for maintenance and repairs.

The first German bombs fell on Plymouth in July 1940, claiming three lives, but much worse was to come in 1941, when the city was all but destroyed. In April 1941, a direct hit on a communal air-raid shelter claimed 76 souls. Most of the city's children were evacuated. When the air-raid signal sounded, those who remained would be loaded into lorries that were driven to safer ground in the wilds of Dartmoor.

Despite the Nazi bombardment, the city of Plymouth persisted, as did HMNB *Devonport*, where my next appointment was situated in a semi-basement building at Mount Wise.

On my first day I was met at the station in Plymouth and taken straight to report to the Port Superintendent WRNS Mrs Welby.

Euphemia Welby, widow of Captain Richard Welby RN, was well-known and very well-respected in Plymouth. She had been a Red Cross cook in Malta during the First World War. Many former Red Cross volunteers had joined the WRNS, encouraged by the example of Dame Katharine Furse. Mrs Welby was appointed to port superintendent in Plymouth in 1939, where she oversaw the recruitment of all the Wrens at HMS *Drake*. A charming portrait of Mrs Welby by Richard Dring can be found in the collection of the Imperial War Museum.

Having met Superintendent Welby, I was quickly introduced to the Operations Room, where I was to be in charge, as plotting officer, of a watch. There were four watches and four Wren ratings to a watch.

The Royal Navy and the RAF Coastal Command shared a single huge operations room at Mount Wise. The area was divided into two even halves, with a vast map covering the wall at the Royal Navy's end, showing the entire Western Approaches including the whole North Atlantic Ocean. At the back of this room and facing the wall map at a raised level sat the senior Royal Navy and RAF officers of the day, who shared the space – with a glass division to separate them from the Operations Room.

Both the navy and Coastal Command had their individual radar plots placed in their own halves, consisting of table cabinets with enlarged maps of the west coast and with all the radar stations marked. The maps were covered in transparent talc, upon which you could draw routes and write the latest information in coloured wax markers, while small models indicating convoys, ships or aircraft were moved accordingly. The four Wren ratings stood by each of the four sides with headphones on to receive reports.

There were numerous radar stations round the coast of the United Kingdom and the operators would telephone regularly to the Wrens to report the latest position of any ships, convoys or unidentified blips which had appeared on their radar screens, all of which were plotted immediately. German E-boats were known to try to creep about our coasts and we could therefore be warned of their presence. These E-boats could be anything from a small armed motorboat to a torpedo boat. The Germans called them 'schnellboot', which means 'fast boat'. They certainly were fast so it was useful to have as much notice as possible of their arrival.

As I was to learn, 'Radar' is an acronym of 'Radio Direction and Ranging'. It is a method of detecting the distance and velocity of all manner of things using radio waves.

The history of radar begins in the late nineteenth century when German physicist Heinrich Hertz noticed that metallic objects reflected radio waves. Hertz's discovery was expanded upon by fellow German Christian Hülsmeyer, who invented the 'Telemobiloskop' or 'Remote Object Viewing Device'. This was soon put into use by ships, to help them navigate in fog. However, not much further progress was made with radar until the 1930s, when the US Naval Research labs found that they were able to detect wave patterns made by both ship and aircraft engines and furthermore work out, by using an oscilloscope and the direction of the antenna, the exact location of any target.

Another major breakthrough came when British physicists John Randall and Harry Boot invented something known as the cavity magnetron, which enabled the use of a short pulse of radio energy, allowing smaller systems to be built. This was invaluable for their deployment around the UK coast at the beginning of the Second World War.

We were taken to visit one of the radar stations at Prawle Point in Devon, which helped one to understand this magic equipment. We learned how a trained operator could quickly distinguish the distance, speed, direction and consistency of an object from the radar signals received. These details would be telephoned to a plotting room Wren who would mark the new information on the plot; thus the operations officers and all concerned could see at a glance the up-to-the-minute position of shipping round the coast.

I was responsible not only for the radar plot but also for the equally important and thrilling huge wall map which showed the positions of any ship or convoy or indeed any reported U-boat in the whole North Atlantic. Information to adjust these came by signal; if there was none, the ship or convoy would be moved on according to its supposed speed by dead reckoning.

Our working hours were as follows: from 1800 to 0900 (15 hours), then from 0900 next day to 1800, with 48 hours off after that. If we were having a quiet night, we might take it in turns to go outside for a breath of fresh air, or to the canteen for something to eat. There were bunks, too, where we could take a short nap, though these were so evil-smelling that I preferred to stay awake and read. In any case, the minute one dozed off was inevitably the moment an admiral would need something from the chart cabinet, for which I was responsible.

Whether anybody but myself knew that I had never been in a plot in my life and had absolutely no idea what I was doing upon my arrival in Plymouth, I never discovered. Plotting was a new category and as yet no official training course was available. In an effort to hide my ignorance, I would ask subtle questions of the other Wren plotters, hoping I would not give myself away. It was fortunate that I had always been very interested in the navy since that glorious moment when as a child I had watched the whole fleet sail into the Grand Harbour in Malta. As a result, I was familiar with the names and capabilities of every ship in the fleet. I was fortunate, also, that my fellow Wrens were very kind and if they guessed that I was occasionally out of my depth, they never said so, instead gently guiding me in the right direction.

There were slow convoys, known as ONS (followed by a designated number) with speed taken from the slowest ship, perhaps five knots, and fast convoys of troop ships – often named HX (followed by a number) – and special cargoes going at maybe 15 knots. Then there were the 'Monsters', the *Queen Mary*, the *Queen Elizabeth, Mauretania, Aquitania, Franconia*, and others which had been luxury liners, now troop ships. The convoys would all be given zigzag routes of various natures and these zigzags each had a number, with pre-arranged changes of course. The convoys would be escorted by destroyers, corvettes, minesweepers, trawlers or anything else available, at speeds from 35 knots to 12 knots or thereabouts. I loved this job of keeping the picture bang up to date, and blessed the inspired moment when I had chosen plotting and so luckily been asked to do it. I and my Wrens felt deeply involved watching this horrific but vital Battle of the Atlantic unfold.

THE BATTLE OF THE ATLANTIC

It was Churchill who coined the phrase 'Battle of the Atlantic'. He claimed in his memoirs that it was the only campaign of the war that gave him sleepless nights. In particular, he said, "the only thing that ever really frightened me during the war was the U-boat peril."

The U-boats – the unterseeboots – were indeed the most worrying of the vessels in the Kriegsmarine.

The fall of France had given Germany a terrible advantage by allowing the Kriegsmarine access to ports on the Atlantic coast where they could establish their U-boat bases. Germany had also increased U-boat production dramatically since the spring of 1941.

At the same time, the Allies continued using convoys to protect merchant traffic. These convoys might contain as many as 60 ships. For a certain distance from the British shoreline, the convoys could also be protected by the RAF. This air cover was picked up by the Canadian Air Force on the other side, but there remained a section in the middle that the airmen couldn't reach. This became known as the Atlantic Gap. Despite this, strange as it sounds, it was harder for the U-boats to find a convoy than it was for them to find a single ship. With the convoys constituting a single entity, there were fewer targets to be found.

Unfortunately, the Germans had at the head of their U-boat fleet an impressive tactician, Admiral Karl Dönitz. Having become a U-boat captain in the First World War, Dönitz dedicated himself to working out how to make the U-boats more effective. He first came up with the idea that the U-boats should hunt the Atlantic in large groups, which would become known as 'wolf packs'.

The idea was that the wolf pack would begin its hunt widely dispersed to cover a greater range but as soon as one U-boat spotted a target, it would send its location to all the other submarines in the 'pack', who would immediately come in for the kill. It was a deadly effective strategy.

Dönitz oversaw the U-boat operations in the Atlantic from his headquarters in France. His orders and the signals between the U-boats were sent in the Enigma code, which the Germans still believed to be unbreakable. The one weak point of Dönitz's strategy was that a wolf pack attack required so much communication. The more signals the submarines sent, the more likely those signals were to be picked up by Allied listening posts. There were several dedicated to just that purpose – listening to the U-boats. They took down the Enigma code messages which were now able to be quickly decoded at Bletchley Park and transformed into signals that we could use in the plotting room.

To be able to decode the U-boats' signals made it much easier for the Allies to anticipate a wolf-pack attack and did help to reduce the number of losses quite significantly, until a period between February and December 1942, known as the Black Out.

During this time the U-boats used a new unreadable key that made it harder to gain vital intelligence. This meant that by the end of 1942, the U-boats were back in force. The Germans were adding new submarines to their fleet at a rate of 20 per month. As a result, Allied losses soared, cutting off vital supplies of food and petrol to Britain. We had to win the Battle of The Atlantic. Losing it would mean losing the war altogether.

ABOARD A MONSTER

Over the years, I have collected a great many interesting stories from my fellow Wrens. As I discovered, at one time the motto of the WRNS had been 'Never At Sea' but that definitely changed after 1939.

My friend Elizabeth, Duchess of Northumberland, was one of the first Wrens to go to sea, as part of the crew of the *Mauretania*, bringing troops back from America in 1943.

The Monsters, as I mentioned before, were the converted liners, which had been pressed into wartime service as troopers, challenging the enemy as they dashed across the oceans at top speed, laden with thousands of our precious American and Canadian forces to Britain, to prepare for the onslaught on D-Day. The liners were manned by their peace-time crew of merchant seamen, who would not have access to military codes, providing another wonderful opportunity to make use of the only too willing Wrens to run the signals office.

The *Mauretania* was launched in 1939; it was a name which brought her predecessor, the legendary and eponymous Blue Riband-holder, to mind, and shortly after the outbreak of war she was converted into a trooper, armed with six-inch guns and painted grey. Her gross tonnage was 35,738, she was 772 ft long by 89 ft beam and her service speed was 23 knots. The two *Queens* (approximately 81,000 and 83,000 tons and averaging 26 knots) and the World War I veteran *Aquitania* (45,647 tons and 23 knots) were similarly converted. The latter was always a favourite of mine with her four splendid funnels and her vast tonnage – she was built in 1914, and at that time was the largest liner in the world. Her passenger accommodation was superior to anything previously seen on the North Atlantic, with a first class drawing room decorated in the Adam style, its walls adorned with prints of English seaports and Royal portraits. The smoking room was modelled on Greenwich Hospital, with oak panelling and beams; the restaurant was reminiscent of Louis XIV, while the grill room was Jacobean in style. She also had very sumptuous passenger cabins, and became one of the best known Cunard liners. I have already described my satisfaction in plotting these marvellous fast monsters, who sailed across the Atlantic without escorts, on carefully planned zigzag courses.

The *Queens*, in addition to a crew of over 1,000, carried sometimes as many as 15,000 troops on each trip, relying on their speed for safety. Diversions of route were not a problem provided the dangers ahead of them could be detected by the Operational Intelligence Centre (OIC) in time (and they were), and although they crossed and recrossed the Atlantic incessantly between 1942 and D-Day and beyond, they were very rarely sighted and not one was lost.

The Duchess sent me this account of the wartime career that took her right around the world.

"Having joined the WRNS in March 1942, I worked as a coder at Chatham – Area Head Quarters in the tunnels. In the summer of 1943 there were rumours that Wrens were now needed at sea in the troop carriers – and that the *Mauretania* was applying for Wren coders. Our signal officer came to tell us this, and I had my name at the top of the page before he stopped talking!

"Next day I was sent for by our commanding officer, who told me that they were about to send me to the Officers' Training Course, and that I would not therefore be eligible for the *Mauretania*. However I pleaded with him and they said they would think about it. I was told the next day that I had won my request! A few weeks later, three of us set off for Liverpool (August Bank Holiday 1943), where we reported to Commander in Chief, Western Approaches. He explained what our lives would be, the duties etc. He then sent for me later on, and told me that my brother's ship was due in Liverpool that evening and that he would give him the message that I was in Liverpool. What a coincidence. He got in touch and I went aboard that evening – and found that his ship HMS *Woodstock* was lying alongside the *Mauretania!* Next day we boarded her, were given our new capbands – 'Cunard White Star' – and shown our cabin for three. The passengers were mostly British officers going on courses to America.

"We sailed that night and went on duty decoding signals, brought to us by the wireless operator – we were working naval watches. Unfortunately one of the girls was terribly seasick all night and we two had to work watch on, watch off. It took us 10 days to America, zigzagging across the Atlantic, arriving at night with New York all lit up, and the Statue of Liberty looking wonderful.

"We were there for a week and though we did some work on codebooks, we were free to go ashore and wander about. The ships' officers, who became our friends, took us out to lunch and dinner in the city. They also insisted that us girls – even though we were only ratings – should be allowed to eat in the officers' dining room.

"For the return journey the ship filled up with with American troops – I think about 700–800, coming to fight with the British. There was not nearly enough accommodation and they just slept where they could – for the 10 days back to Liverpool.

"Our next trip was to Boston, Massachusetts, and the last two to Halifax, Nova Scotia – where it was getting quite wintry. One of these ships' signals came in from a Naval Escort Group, (which happened to be my brother's) saying they had sighted a U-boat and a few signals later on, they had sunk it!

"On returning to Liverpool each time, we had nearly a week's leave. We were only supposed to do three trips before being replaced, but one of us had to stay on for another trip to teach the new Wrens – and I was the lucky one!

"When my time came to leave the *Mauretania*, the ships' officers gave a farewell party for me in a little pub on the quayside – I left in tears (I loved that ship!).

"My only other adventures in the war were my journeys to and from Australia, arriving January 1945 and leaving in December 1945. By this time I had got my commission (Third Officer Scott!). The trip took about a month – 10 days by sea to New York in the *Aquitania* – with 10 other Wrens, four days by train across America, 10 days waiting in San Francisco for transport across the Pacific. Finally by seaplanes stopping off for two nights in Honolulu, one night on a small island, three nights in the New Hebrides – looked after by Australian bomber pilots and New Zealand fighter pilots! A wonderful journey for someone who had hardly ever left England.

"The journey back to England at the end of the year was by sea in the *Aquitania* from Sydney via South Africa, taking four weeks, spending Christmas Day in Cape Town, and invited that night with three friends to a party on Table Mountain. We arrived back in England in Southampton in the bleak midwinter, mid January 1946."

The then Third Officer Scott, now Elizabeth, Duchess of Northumberland, finished her accompanying letter by saying:

"Trying to keep my story as brief as possible, I forgot to mention what we actually did in Australia! I was stationed in Melbourne and worked as a signals officer in the Royal Naval Headquarters, Melbourne. I happened to be on duty the night and early morning when the signal came through that "Peace had been declared in Europe". What a thrill!! But there was only the signal officer at that moment to tell it to! I had a very happy time in Australia and arranged to see quite a bit of it with weekend leaves to Sydney, Canberra and Adelaide, even a trip to a farm in the Outback."

This sensational career of service in the WRNS with so much exciting sea time and travel must constitute a record – who could imagine that joining up would bring such lucky chances, seized without hesitation and with both hands. One should not however forget the courage which inspired these instant volunteers; they would know the risks very well and be prepared to face what was one of the most deadly periods of that dangerous arena of conflict, the Battle of the Atlantic, seething with U-boats whose skilled and determined captains, equipped with the latest new and ingenious weapons, could have lost us the war – and very nearly did.

OFF-DUTY

While the work we were doing in the plotting room in Plymouth was deadly serious, we did still find time to enjoy ourselves off duty.

We lived in quite reasonable terraced houses out of town at Mannamead, which had been an affluent suburb of the city at the end of the 19th century. Public transport was pretty dire at the time; for some reason all the buses seemed to be planned to just miss whatever you were trying to catch. I remember making a vow that if ever I had a chance to revenge myself on a Plymouth bus driver I would certainly do so. He would only have to see you hurrying to catch his bus for him to put his foot down and speed away, leaving you almost weeping with frustration and rage in the freezing gale, hoping that something really nasty would overtake him.

By now there were occasional courses laid on for Wrens and I was sent to Bath to do one. What it was about remains a mystery, but I do remember that on the return journey I missed my train. How I came to do this I can't imagine, as one of my many failings is to be always frightfully early for everything. This trait I think must be hereditary because I remember my father describing how in his youth, his family went on a journey by train. Incredibly, the horse-drawn coach, complete with passengers and luggage, was made to do a dress rehearsal to the station the day before!

I definitely didn't go as far as that, but having missed the train it was a despairing moment and I could not believe my luck when I was saved by a delightful Polish officer with whom I had been consorting at a party the night before. He astonished me by saying, "Shall I take you back in the old crate?"

"What old crate?"

I was nearly speechless when I realised he meant his aeroplane. I stammered out my rapturous acceptance!

This episode may sound quite ordinary now but then it was quite the most daring episode in my life. My rescuer was, I suppose, an instructor because he had at his disposal a Miles Magister training plane, with just two seats, one behind the other – in the open air of course. I had to sit on my parachute in the back and we set off in fine style looking out for and overtaking the train I had missed. My pilot tried to give me some good frights en route and make the trip extra thrilling by dive bombing cows or anything else that took his fancy. I had been hoping that he might loop the loop for an extra show off, but perhaps it was just as well that he didn't, or I might have fallen out. Flying in an open plane, low down over the River Tamar and seeing the whole estuary and coast as on a map, was an experience I'd like to relive even today.

There were lots of parties in Plymouth, many of them in ships. I had experienced wonderful gatherings during my family's time in

Malta when my father was captain of HMS *Shropshire*. The parties I went to in Plymouth were of a very different calibre, but they were never to be forgotten.

My Wren friends and I made some amazing friends with some submariners, many of whom were based in Devonport. This was my first introduction to this secret, underwater, dangerous world, which seemed to attract a unique and brave breed of man.

Submarine crews are the pick of the navy, for this highly-specialised service offers fine opportunities for individual derring-do – the dauntless spirit that animated our sailors of old. They are the hidden eyes and ears of the navy, able to lurk undetected, observing enemy movements, able to hear the slightest distant whirr of machinery, by catching the sound waves, using the hull of the submerged submarine as a giant hydrophone. (This acts rather on the principle of a stethoscope.)

Parties in submarines were particularly special, as apart from the excitement of going aboard one of these esoteric vessels, space was at a premium and the tiny wardroom was very cosy. Whenever possible on Saturday nights, we would go for drinks on board, before going on to Genoni's, an Italian restaurant near Drake's Circus, or to the Moreland Links Hotel, out near Yelverton, where we danced the night away. We always wore long evening dresses, although my friend Eve Lindsay and I had very few of these, and used to borrow from each other to ring the changes.

Another friend, Ruby Cortez, had some lovely clothes. Ruby was a ball of fire. Before becoming a Wren, she had been secretary to Alexander Korda, the British-Hungarian film producer and director who set up his own studio, where he made such famous films as *The Private Life of Henry VIII* and *The Thief of Baghdad*. In 1942, he was awarded a knighthood for his contribution to the war effort. Post-war he would go on to make *The Third Man*, a film believed by many to be the best British film of all time.

It could be quite difficult to climb on and off a submarine in a full-length dress but we did it as elegantly as we could. One famous evening, Steve, who was the paymaster on board HMS *Rorqual*, suggested that as we were so tired of our same old dresses, why not wear their dinner jackets for a change? This brilliant idea took some organising – and it is impossible to imagine the contortions necessary when they tied our bow ties...

HMS *RORQUAL*

HMS *Rorqual* was our favourite host ship. She was a big mine-laying submarine that had just returned from two years' active service in the Mediterranean. She was brought to Devonport for a refit in February 1942.

Rorqual is the name given to the group of baleen whales that includes the blue whale, the largest of them all, and the submarine's badge showed one of those magnificent creatures, floating in a blue background, with a gold crown atop.

By the time I came to know her, HMS *Rorqual* had already had a distinguished war. The Mediterranean campaign was the most significant Royal Navy submarine campaign of the conflict, making a big contribution to allied operations in North Africa and the invasions of Sicily and Italy.

It was dangerous work. 25 Royal Navy submarines were lost in the course of the campaign. Yet though they did a tremendous job in incredibly difficult conditions, the Royal Navy's submariners were not fêted in the same way as the RAF aces were back then.

Rorqual had claimed several Italian boats and a German troop transport. As well as laying mines and attacking enemy shipping, she had been used to move supplies from Beirut and Alexandria to Malta, which was under siege. These missions were known as 'magic carpet runs', with *Rorqual* carrying medical supplies and vital fuel for the RAF fighter planes and mail for the servicemen. She also carried some passengers back and forth.

The captain of HMS *Rorqual* at that time was Lennox Napier, a descendant of John Napier, inventor of Napierian logarithms and the decimal point. Like my father, Lennox came from a naval family and was so certain the naval life was for him that he went to the Britannia Royal Naval College in Dartmouth at the age of 13. He then served on HMS *Nelson*, the flagship of the Home Fleet, before deciding that he would prefer to volunteer for submarines.

Though *Rorqual* was in Plymouth for just a short period of time, Lennox and I quickly became great friends. As well as spending those entertaining evenings together in the submarine's wardroom and out on the town, we used to walk miles over Dartmoor, discussing everything under the sun. We never came to any conclusion about the future, which seemed far away and insecure, but somehow I thought that when the war was won, and if we were both still alive, we would meet again. I always felt Lennox came from that rather romantic genre of man who would not commit himself to any course of action he could not be sure of carrying out.

Lennox rarely talked about what he had been doing; it was all very hush-hush and although I knew what a distinguished war he had had, I only discovered some of the details when he died recently and his son Christopher Napier, himself a submariner, wrote a book about his father's career. I found out why Lennox had been awarded both the DSO and the DSC.

Over the course of the war, *Rorqual* laid a total of 1,599 mines in the Mediterranean but it was Lennox's skill that made her a deadly adversary. One of the enemy ships Lennox's mines destroyed was the *Ankara*, which was transporting tanks to Rommel's troops in North Africa. Another was the *Wilhelmsburg*, a tanker which was also carrying valuable military equipment. The *Rorqual* took the *Wilhelmsburg* out with a torpedo. This loss apparently caused Hitler to lose his temper with his Grand Admiral Karl Dönitz. Lennox was very amused to hear this and almost considered having enraged the Führer to be a far greater accolade than either of his medals.

THE PERISHERS

I can only imagine the amazement and shock on the face of a hardened submarine captain such as Lennox Napier, having been selected to attend the legendary 'Perishers' course at HMS *Dolphin*, upon finding out he was to be instructed by what he would consider 'a chit of a girl', a Wren.

The 'Perishers' course, held at Fort Blockhouse, the submarine HQ at Gosport, was the acme of a submariner's career. Commanding officers of submarines were placed under intense pressure, and tested to their mental, physical and psychological limits, but even already experienced ones had to be handpicked for this highly esteemed refresher course using the newest, up-to-the moment-techniques.

The candidate's astonishment that the course would be delivered by a Wren would be quickly replaced by surprised respect for the remarkable capability of the young women. They were trained by Commander Howard Francis Bone, a renowned submarine commander himself, who had made the name HMS *Tigris* feared in enemy circles by sinking 11 ships with an aggregate displacement of 38,500 tons, for which he was awarded the DSO and Bar and the DSC and Bar. It was Commander Bone who first had the idea that Wrens could replace male instructors and man the control table at the simulator known as the Attack Teacher.

Hazel Russell (née Hough) was introduced to me when I was on my quest for wartime Wrens who had experienced interesting careers. I asked if she had ever told her unique story to anyone before and she said no one had ever been interested. She also pointed out that when one was sworn to secrecy, as we were, for years after the war you could almost forget yourself what had happened so long ago. Nevertheless, she was able to give me this account of her time at HMS *Dolphin*.

"In 1941 I was 21 and a fully trained secretary, employed by an insurance company. In my spare time I drove a YMCA van to anti-aircraft gun and balloon defence sites in the North London area. Since I wanted to join the services I decided to volunteer to join the WRNS and hoped that I could become a driver. I was accepted and arrived in Portsmouth in September to do two weeks' general training. I was then given a driving test and to my surprise was told that I had failed and they tried to persuade me to become a typist.

"HMS *Dolphin*, the submarine base in Portsmouth harbour, had a simulator known as the Attack Teacher and fortunately they were considering the possibility of recruiting six Wrens to replace the sailors who manned it. The Attack Teacher was used to complete the training of first lieutenants to become 'Perishers' (trained captains), and experienced captains went back to learn the latest tactics and details of potential targets. The normal male crew was to be posted to sea and the plan was to find out whether

Wrens could replace them; I, with one other girl, was chosen to see whether after three weeks' training we could take over.

"The instructor, Commander H.F. Bone, a very distinguished submarine captain, decided we were competent, and I, having been made Leading Wren, together with five other Wrens, became the crew in November 1941.

"The simulator was housed in a building on the *Dolphin* quay and had two floors: the lower one known as the control room had a rotating conning tower with a periscope and various instruments including a gramophone playing underwater noises. The most important instrument was the 'fruit machine' which was a mechanical analogue computer; this was fed with target information, submarine depth etc, and worked out the torpedo firing conditions. The upper floor had mechanisms to control the movement of the model targets along a rail track some fifty yards long. In addition, in this room there was a large plotting table on which the torpedo tracks were recorded for critical analysis. The models were all very tiny but accurate replicas of enemy shipping, and were kept up to date throughout the war and of course, were subject to tight security.

"The whole complex was Top Secret and had to be manned at night by two Wrens which meant that I slept on board every third night. There was, in addition to the main room on the lower floor where the courses were carried out, a small room which contained two camp beds and very limited facilities. This was our accommodation which we used generally and when we were on 'watch'. The *Dolphin* canteen was a considerable distance away and when on duty we sometimes preferred to turn our electric stove on its back and heat soup and make scrambled eggs, made from tinned egg powder.

"The officers' training lasted six weeks, three with us and the other three at sea. During the three weeks before the next course arrived, we carried out all the maintenance: the cleaning, polishing and scrubbing necessary to satisfy our very critical commander. This work was carried out by the six Wrens, as no other personnel were allowed into the facility. These three weeks were also when leave was taken, and in addition we were available to carry out other duties to help the establishment.

"When the new course arrived, the commander addressed them and told them they were about to learn the very latest techniques to be used in carrying out an attack on an enemy ship. This covered the approach to a firing position which was recorded on the plotting table in detail, together with the actual firing point of the torpedoes, and after each attack was made, the results were analysed and discussed.

"At the end of each course, Commander Bone expected the officers to take us six Wrens out to dinner over the water to Southsea, to show their appreciation of the hard work and support we had given them on their course. On one occasion when we missed the 'Jolly Boat' back, and were locked out of our quarters at Alverstoke, we were punished by having to peel potatoes for three weeks.

"When *Taku*, a T-class submarine, came to *Dolphin* and her officers attended our refresher course, they were invited to a dance at our quarters at Alverstoke. During the evening we chided them, saying that we Wrens, having been through dozens of attacks, could achieve more hits on enemy targets than they could. They answered jokingly, 'Why don't you come out to sea and show us?' I replied that we would like the challenge, but when their captain,

Commander Pitt, was asked for permission, he laughed and said that if it was sanctioned from above, he would gladly take us!

"The next day, I approached Commander Bone, who agreed that we deserved to go, but said that I would have to see Admiral Darke, the commanding officer of *Dolphin*, and get his agreement. I then saw the Chief Wren Officer who obtained an appointment with him. When the day arrived, I was extremely nervous, but the Admiral put me at ease and said that he had received glowing reports of our work, and that he would give his agreement providing we strictly adhered to his conditions. These were: that the exercise would be Top Secret; that we would embark before daylight and on returning would disembark in a discreet manner; and for obvious reasons would wear bell-bottom trousers.

"Number One, (the First Officer) of *Taku*, who made all the rearrangements necessary for his crew of about 50 men to accommodate us on a temporary basis, greeted us six rather nervous Wrens aboard before the sun rose. We were made very welcome and soon got used to the odours and cramped conditions. Commander Pitt arrived and we cast off and sailed down the Solent, on the surface, out into the English Channel. We were given a tour of the boat and saw all that went on in each department, and I was enormously impressed by the size of the torpedoes. We then spent a lot of time in the control room, where we were much more familiar with the equipment.

"We cruised around on the surface waiting for the target ship to arrive for the torpedo-firing exercise, and during this wait each Wren went up into the conning tower and looked out across the water for any signs of activity. When our target arrived in the exercise area, we dived to periscope depth which was about 25 ft. In turn, we each looked through the periscope at the target and, with the ship's crew casting a watchful eye on us, we assisted the Number One Officer to carry out the first attack. When he fired the dummy torpedo it was a direct hit. Then I took over and manoeuvred the boat into a firing position and fired. The first torpedo missed, but the second was a hit, and I shouted 'Down periscope!' and the captain took us down to 'safety'. Everyone was delighted with the result of the exercise.

"We then surfaced, and the officers gave up their tiny ward-room for us to have a tot and a splendid lunch. The captain told us that the CPO chef had spent the entire morning organising a sumptuous meal of roast beef, Yorkshire pudding and vegetables followed by an exotic sweet. After thanking the captain and his officers for taking us out and giving us such a thrilling day, we returned to base, tired but very pleased to have had the privilege of going to sea in a submarine. And when finally ashore, we swore to keep secret our special exercise, and what we had seen in one of His Majesty's operational submarines.

"Working with these officers meant that we Wrens knew them well by the end of the three weeks, and had a good understanding of the dangers they were about to face. Normally they went into combat waters when they left us, and naturally their leaving left us concerned. The loss of one of our boats, especially if it had been captained by one of our course members, was a thoroughly depressing event for us."

Hazel and her team must be among very few Wrens to have had such a wonderful chance; I can't imagine anything more thrilling than to actually go to sea, submerge in an operational submarine, and then be able with all her experience and training to fire the torpedo and hit, and finally to be allowed to give the order 'Down periscope!' It must have been the apogee of her ambitions.

LETTERS FROM LENNOX

I remained at Plymouth until July 1942 when the whole headquarters moved up to Liverpool. It had been decided that the
Western Approaches would be plotted from there while Plymouth
Command took a more localised role, concentrating on protecting
the south-west coastline.

I did not follow my team to Liverpool but was instead sent
to HMS *Cochrane* in Scotland, for plotting duties and to act as the
naval liaison officer at Turnhouse, which is now Edinburgh's main
airport. I lived in a hotel in the city and my room was at the top of
a great number of stairs. I remember one day waking up feeling
frightfully ill. I briefly considered calling in sick, but decided that by
the time I had walked all the way down the stairs to the telephone,
I might as well go in.

After a couple of days of this, I had a visit from my mother,
who was horrified to find me with a bright red face and covered in
spots. It turned out that I had been soldiering on through a bout of
German measles. Needless to say, neither my superiors nor the hotel
manager were very pleased to hear the news. I had to quarantine

with my mother in my hotel room until I recovered enough to go back home to Scotland to finish my recuperation there.

When Lennox and I went our separate ways, with me leaving for Edinburgh and the *Rorqual* due to set sail for Malta in June 1942, we promised we would write. There were few telephones in those days and we certainly weren't allowed to use them for personal calls without very good reason. Emails were yet to be invented. Letters were the only way to keep in touch.

Lennox wrote wonderfully funny letters which he illustrated with skilful cartoons. I kept many of them and was glad to be able to pass some of them on to his son, Christopher, to be put in the appendix of his book about his father's war.

When we were first parted, Lennox wrote the following:

"I hope you are going to write to me from time to time. This is good for morale of persons in Foreign Parts and even if distasteful, may be counted as war work and therefore highly virtuous."

Indeed, writing to people in the services was considered to be very good for the war effort. Guidelines were issued at a national level, reminding people to write only about happy things, in order to keep their readers' spirits up. We also had to be very careful not to write about the specifics of our work, for fear that secret information might fall into the wrong hands. For that reason, all post sent to or from military establishments had to pass the censors, who would vet each letter for security purposes. I imagine that being a censor could sometimes be a very interesting job for someone with an active imagination.

One of Lennox's early missives to me, written shortly after I must have left for Scotland, is a perfect example of a morale-boosting letter. I'm not sure when it arrived, since the post in those days was not terribly reliable. Letters to anyone serving in the navy had to be directed via the GPO in London. Lennox started writing the letter while he was still in Plymouth, painting the town red with our joint friends.

HMS Rorqual
c/o GPO London

My dear Christian,

This is to wish you farewell – Empire or otherwise according to taste. "Ave atque vale*" as we say in our usual affected manner: (This has got in because I have been reading Tacitus – about that dear Caligula, such a nice man).

You might hardly credit it but I went off yesterday evening, being Saturday, to a certain well-known hotel with Steve, Eve, Ruby and others: this time was really the last though. It gives me particular pleasure to announce that, on returning, Ruby in person was soundly censured by one of her messmates for making too much noise.

Don't imagine however that we have been enjoying the fleshpots ever since you left. We have been places meanwhile. One place we went was both unintentional and dramatic. We were steaming through a certain Narrows and Rocky Place with a local Pilot in charge. While passing the lighthouse so close that the lighthouse keeper not only could, but did, spit on to the upper deck, we suddenly began to go sharply uphill and finally came to rest with a grinding crunch. At this point the pilot, with the famous last words "Oh xxxx it" on his lips passed clean away into the arms of the Signalman, thus most successfully, but unsportingly, leaving me with the onus of extricating the whole organisation from a predicament for which he was entirely responsible. This we managed. But the Pilot's bowler hat, which fell over the side in the general turmoil, was last seen being worn by a porpoise, disporting itself around the ship's bows. At least so a Leading Stoker declared, though the man in question is notoriously unreliable. The beast he said had exceptionally beautiful eyelashes.

This morning I was paid a visit by the Old Guard, who were shown round the boat, so choc-a-bloc with boxes and stores, trunks, potatoes and pistons that after an extended obstacle race, with all participants glowing freely at the end of it, I do not really think they had seen anything at all. Ruby said afterwards that she now understood why people found service in submarines so absorbing. So Heaven knows what idea she has got in her head or is now going to spread about in an unsuspecting world.

I take it by this time, your two Commanders, if not the RAF, will have been set well on the road to being brought to heel. I cannot help hoping that they are that type of Commander you have been used to dealing with in these parts. This kind – if you catch my meaning.

A man is practising the banjulele in the next room of this hotel. This is too much – I can't go on.

Love Lennox.

*Hail and Farewell.

A little later Lennox and the *Rorqual* were in the Mediterranean and he sent a letter from Beirut, which the Allies had retaken in 1941 and were using as a base. As you will see, the letter reached me in a very roundabout sort of way, which was typical of the time.

It was very hard to keep a correspondence going in war time.

HMS Rorqual,
22nd September [1942]

My dear Christian

We are now installed in our new home – and very nice it is, I must say. We live in a large and commodious house, once the property of Russian hermits. I must confess I had always imagined hermits to be austere, ascetic gentlemen, living in caves in the mountains. But not at all. Asceticism is strikingly absent from the home and the flesh is only seriously mortified by the marked inadequacy of the bathing arrangements – a state of affairs which I strongly suspect did not mortify the Russians in the least.

One other cross, indeed, we do have to bear and that is the immediate proximity of the so-called Fighting French. There appears to be only one all-important aspect of French Military training and that is bugling. At 0500 it starts with one instructor playing (a note) then every recruit plays (a note), some a little sharp and some a little flat. Then the instructor plays (two notes) and the recruits follow suit. All day long, with no pause, they stick at it, until about 1900 they have reached (twelve notes) after which, thank God, they stop. And so to work again at 0500 the next morning. But what, after all, does that matter when we are living in a lovely country, where rationing is unheard of (by us), where I am supplied with a motor car and chauffeur at the public expense and where, in between patrols, I am sent to cool off 3,000 feet up in the mountains.

French is the language of our daily intercourse. This comes a trifle hard anyway after long years of disuse but what really upsets me is that I am informed, not only by one person or by two, but by all whom I meet, that I speak the language in the most perfect German accent. However, since no one here has heard more than vague rumours of there being some kind of war, or at least some marked divergence of opinion, between the powers in the great world outside, this does not really matter. Truly the people, at least the village people, round about are embarrassingly friendly. As one goes for one's Saturday afternoon walk in the hills one is pressed on every side – to go into this cottage for a cup of coffee or to accept a great bunch of grapes from the vine growing over the door of that one. In short we live in a kind of arcadia with Bugling. What, of course, makes it even more arcadian for me at the moment is that on the second day in harbour my entire wardrobe was removed by an enterprising Burglar while the laundryman was engaged in enjoying his siesta. The simplicity of attire compelled by this disaster should perhaps be called Spartan rather than arcadian, and in any case is not altogether unsuited to the climate.

(Pay no attention to the pictures I put in. They are only to keep up morale which is liable to become reduced to a particularly low level by the rigours of letter writing.)

Naturally in this Eden there are nymphs and shepherdesses and what have you. The best we can do in this line at present is a small female cypher staff who live in our mess. This, I must tell you at once, does not really add all it might to the idyllic scene, chiefly on account of the presence among them of the local General's wife – a charming lady no doubt but one whose continual presence in the wardroom fills me with the utmost alarm and despondency. Particularly is this so since there is no getting from my cabin to the bathroom except by going *through the mess. The disadvantages of this layout are apparent, and as I scurry past furtively, on my way to my evening scrub, loofah in hand, and all too inadequately clad for communing with Generals' wives, I get the iciest stare from the good lady who has a most unhappy predilection for a seat immediately outside my door.*

I am afraid that you may hardly believe me when I tell you that we have now, really, acquired a violin for our wardroom. (A present from a gentleman who could not take all his luggage home, which he insisted in pressing upon my Engineer Officer in spite of the most vehement protestations that he had no use for the instrument.) The Bluebells of Scotland has so far been practised (and that pizzicato owing to restrictions of space which make bowing difficult) and it has been decided that actual performances of this classic are to be reserved for the occasions of one of our operational successes, when it will be rendered by myself, as a kind of paean on the ancient Greek model. As a matter of fact we have had a slight opening success but, by the time the depth charges had ceased pattering about our ears, it must be confessed that the Bluebells had come to be somehow overlooked. Next time, however, there shall be no mistake.

I know you are in fact keeping my morale up as promised, and that it is simply ill fortune that all your letters get sunk or shot down en route (as a matter of fact, as I have not had a single letter since we left home, I am not really complaining at all).

Wishing you, in conclusion, a Merry Michaelmas and a Happy Lord Mayor's Day.

Lots of love,

Lennox

P.S. After setting out on its travels about Sept 22nd this letter has circumnavigated Africa and reached me again circa April 15th in an envelope somewhat embarrassingly addressed "Lennox" HMS Rorqual. *As I am however incurably lazy I have no compunction whatever in sending it off once more on its way, thus relieving me of the necessity of thinking of anything new to say. Besides it still appears to me a fine piece of English Prose and you might as well know what we were up to in September. Suffice it to say we are in no arcadia now.*

> *Love Lennox*
> *HMS* Rorqual *17 April 1943*

Letters overlapped with some reaching their target before letters sent weeks or months earlier. It was easy to think that your pen-pal had forgotten you, then several of those precious pale blue airmail envelopes would arrive at once. And with everyone moving around so often, sometimes one might go on writing to the wrong address for weeks.

Once I had recovered from the German measles, I was sent to HMS *Calliope*, a training establishment in Gateshead, County Durham, in a flat grey building near the Tyne Bridge. Unfortunately, I didn't warm to Newcastle – the watch pattern there meant that I never had time to socialise and make new friends, who might have made getting to know the city more interesting – and so I put in for a transfer as soon as I was able.

I was offered a return to Plymouth or a posting in Belfast. I didn't see much point in returning to Plymouth, since all my friends from there had long since moved on. I also wanted to be involved plotting the Western Approaches again and Plymouth was no longer the place for that. So having never been to Northern Ireland, I decided to plump for another new adventure and said I would like to go to Belfast. Though I wrote to let Lennox know, it would be a long time before he got the news. Thus, when letters finally arrived where they were supposed to, it made them doubly important. They were read and re-read again and again and carefully saved, such as this one from 1943.

HMS Rorqual
10th February 1943

My dear Christian

How nice to hear from you after all these months. I have just got a letter from you – dated 14th September – nevertheless this leads me to hope there may be others, spread around in Space-Time, which will be rolling in slowly, but steadily, long after the outbreak of Peace. I wonder if my letters to you, of which I must ask you to believe there have been several, are also arriving after a similar interval, or at all, for they have been all addressed to Edinburgh where I suppose you have not been at all. Never mind, it is the Kind Thought which is really important, they say.

We have long since left that Garden of Eden in which we started our career abroad and are now in a very sorry, though slowly improving, quarters. Such trifling things as the rain coming through the roof and a total lack of hot water are such everyday matters that they are no longer noticed.

I have however been provided with a new cabin. Into this, by a most ingenious arrangement, is blown a continuous shower of soot through an inaccessible ventilator which takes its supply from a neighbouring chimney – life in fact is exactly like a continuous residence in a Railway station in which there is only corned beef and dry bread in the Buffet and the conveniences are out of order.

The austerity of our daily fare was well summed up the other day by a sailor whom I happened to overhear as he finished the tinned plums which had formed part of his lunch and, by means of the stones, endeavoured to ascertain what he was going to get for supper. As he pushed each stone to the side of his plate he was reciting "Corned Beef, Pressed Beef, Tinned Beef, Beef."

You might suppose that I am having a moan and that Morale is Bad. On the contrary it is very good. (Touching Wood) The war has not been going too badly lately – indeed you may even have seen some highly garbled accounts of our doings in the Press.

Yesterday I had to do a lecture on Submarine Warfare to a large party of soldiers. On arriving on the platform the local military chieftain introduced me as Lieut-Colonel Napier which completely unnerved me and left the whole audience tittering. Later I told a grossly exaggerated funny story of one of our one-time soldier passengers, only to discover too late that he was MO of the regiment and actually in the audience. He now keeps coming to our mess and asking for me – Oh dear!

There is precious little room on these damn things, these bits o paper. I will write you a better letter later. In the meantime

Lots of love

Lennox

Lennox wrote again in March of the same year. He may have been in Algiers at the time though the flora he describes sounds closer to that found in Lebanon, where HMS *Rorqual* would have been at the time of the October letter to which he refers.

HMS Rorqual
c/o GPO

29th March

My dear Christian,

How satisfactory that we have at last established communication. I should have a great deal to tell you about the last six months really but, alas, I can never do it, for fear that an earlier letter may turn up, with a totally different version of the same story. The deplorable habit of improving events for publication may in such cases find me out.

You may hardly believe it but since I last wrote to you I have had three days of the most glorious skiing. This in a country that I have already described to you at some length (vide my 17.10.42, now about at Cape Town) and which is an absolute Heaven in this troubled world. For not only can one go skiing but almost every other human pleasure is provided — you can stuff yourself to the epiglottis with everything that you have almost forgotten about I expect, from oranges to oysters, the shops are full and the country is one of the most beautiful places I have ever seen. Below the snow line the flowers were almost beyond belief, although spring had hardly begun — solid masses of poppies between the olive trees, gentians, anemones, wild cyclamen and cherry and God knows how many I have no idea of the name of. Now we are all back in the hard world again, after only four days of this, but at least every corner of the submarine is packed to capacity with chocolate, razor blades, ivory, apes and peacocks against the bad times to come.

I cannot forbear to repeat one item of news. That is that we acquired a violin, a present from a fleeing evacuee, and on Christmas Day I gave a stirring rendition of the "Bluebells" in the presence of my Petty Officers, meanwhile my Gunlayer, a more competent fiddler than myself, persisted in playing the "Road To The Isles" under the slightly alcoholic impression that he was accompanying me. Probably very bad for discipline, but I think no one had any very clear recollection of the events next day, This is perfectly true. There was no lurverly blonde present.

Lots of love Lennox

Usual address
28 April [1943]

My dear Christian,

How can you do such an absurd thing as apply for Foreign Service? All these places are a pretty fearful bore nowadays. I'm beginning to think of moving in the other direction. High authority has already decreed the day of my return home and, although the same High authority keeps shifting the date just a little further away, yet nevertheless I am, like a schoolboy, already at work on my calendar crossing off the days to the end of term and praying, like the most optimistic kind of schoolboy, that some miraculous intervention, as an earthquake for an example, may strike the school flat and cause the holidays to begin rather sooner than expected. It is not in my experience that this ever happened.

We have been working quite hard lately so recountable news is scarce. The chief incident of our last patrol however, must not be overlooked. Which was that the rats successfully gnawed right through the Coxswain's braces while he was asleep. As we have now a kind of blood-sucking bug onboard to add to our old friends the rats, cockroaches, fleas and woodlice, the struggle for Existence is becoming one of ever-growing intensity.

I can hardly contain my pride today for I have just received a letter from one of my female admirers (married) asking me not only to be the Godfather of her projected infant but declaring her intention of naming it after me should it prove the right variety. Since when I keep finding myself preening myself in front of my mirror (which is only partially covered in soot) and, with a smile of smug complacency, adjusting my now threadbare, but irreplaceable, tie at a more exactly satisfactory angle. Which reminds me for some reason of a rather nice advertisement in the local paper the other day. Translated, it went roughly like this – "For Sale – Comfortable well-upholstered sofa-divan or willing exchange for perambulator in good condition."

My sister keeps sending me books – by every mail yet another volume of "War and Peace." I shall have to read them or be found out ultimately.

I should have thought Ulster was foreign enough for anyone, it would be for me.

Lots of love Lennox

This last letter from Lennox was sent at a moment when I was going through a very exciting time in Belfast, but because the mail took so long and was so unreliable, he hadn't yet heard the news.

Lennox's letters are the only material items apart from my Wren officer's cap badge that I have as souvenirs from the war. I find they portray vividly, through a porthole as it were, the picture of half a relationship. One never forgets old friends such as these.

Belfast 1942, Christian front row on far right

BELFAST

Having chosen to go to Northern Ireland, I was appointed to run the plot at Belfast Castle where the Royal Navy had installed their HQ. I arrived there late in 1942.

Like Plymouth, Belfast had suffered for its role as a naval base. In the April and May of 1941, it had been subjected to a blitz. Unfortunately, bad weather meant that the Luftwaffe missed what might have been described as its 'legitimate' targets, instead dropping bombs on some of the city's most densely populated areas. More than 1,000 people were killed, while 100,000 were left homeless.

The Luftwaffe knew what I would come to learn – Belfast was extremely strategically important to the Allied efforts to win the war at sea.

The Castle itself overlooked the city from the slopes of Cave Hill. The first castle on the site was built by the Normans in the late 12th century. That was succeeded by a stone and timber building in the 17th century, which burned down a hundred years later. It wasn't until the mid-19th century that the building I would come to know was erected on the same spot by the Third Marquis of

Donegall. It was of the Scottish baronial style, made popular after Queen Victoria built Balmoral.

The plotting room was high in the castle, with a good view of Belfast Lough so that we could see the ships coming and going. The radar plot was in the middle of the room and there was a wall plot of the Western Approaches and the whole Atlantic, as there had been in Plymouth. Next door to us and connected by a hatch was the cypher room, and all the signals (uncoded) were handed through to us as they came in.

The Commander in Chief had moved his operations room from Plymouth to Liverpool, while we in Belfast were kept informed of everything that was happening by signal and teleprinter, so we had an accurate and up-to-date picture for visiting officers.

Meanwhile, we recorded the many ships coming up the Irish Sea and from Liverpool and Glasgow, to assemble for the huge slow convoys or the smaller faster ones which formed up to the north, off the west coast of Scotland, near a rocky outcrop called Rockall. Many of the escort ships, destroyers, corvettes and minesweepers were based at Londonderry, and would chase around the vast array of merchant ships like trial sheepdogs, getting them organised in time to sail. A convoy might have as many as 60 ships with two or three corvettes and perhaps one destroyer in attendance. There would have to be a complete blackout and the whole convoy would have to travel at the speed of its slowest ship, which might be no more than five knots.

There was always a senior officer of the day (also working in watches) and I particularly recall a certain night when one of them, who always slept soundly on the floor under his desk, was absolutely impossible to wake up, and this night there was a real emergency: a ship, coming north, was steering far too close to the shore. I wanted to send it a warning signal because of its dangerous position and needed his authority to do so. We pulled him out, sat him up, patted his face, even threw water over him, but he slept on. So I sent the signal anyway.

The endless black nights of the Atlantic and the terrible weather loaded the dice towards our enemy. In our Castle plot we moved the shipping on their known course and speed with the greatest anxiety, dreading the first signal which announced a U-boat sighting or attack – worse still, we worried about many of their escorts and crews.

Being in Ireland was eye-opening after three years of war spent in England and Scotland. Unlike in England, where food was strictly rationed, there was plenty of food in Belfast. We were close to the border and thus it was easy to get anything that we could not find in Ulster from the Republic.

The Royal Navy ships that passed through would always take the opportunity to stock up on what they called 'rabbits', by which they meant those luxury items that were rationed back home. We Wrens would also make occasional sorties to Dublin by train for the same purpose.

I often made the trip with my friends Betty Crudas (née Ashcroft) and Norisse Whitehead (née Ford). Though we could always get enough to eat in Belfast, the food in Dublin was much more variable and we would have a meal every two hours or so, not to waste such a valuable opportunity. Between meals we would go shopping, making the most of the choice in Dublin's stores.

If you bought any clothes, you had to decide whether to wear them or pack them as the customs were very strict on the train home. You were sometimes taken off the train and searched, thus making one late for work. We had our tricks though. We used to hang our shopping bags on the handle outside the carriage where the customs officer did not always think of looking, or one might sit on a small parcel to conceal it. In this way I was once able to smuggle home a box of cigars.

We had quite a busy social life. Ships of the convoy escorts were often sent into Belfast for repairs and on such a chance occasion a fleet destroyer of the Tribal class, called HMS *Oribi*, came in with storm damage. An oribi is a small South African antelope and HMS *Oribi* was so named because her building had been sponsored by the South African government.

She had, of course, her naval priorities correctly aligned and one of her first actions was to send to Belfast Castle for a contingent of Wrens to join the wardroom just as soon as the sun was over the yardarm. There was no lack of volunteers and I was among those who went on this blind date which had lifelong consequences for me.

It was on this auspicious night that I met First Lieutenant John Bruce Lamb DSC. In fact, this was the start of a whirlwind romance, which ended 10 days later with our becoming engaged.

MY FIANCÉ

Naturally our engagement called for a monumental celebration and John, in his capacity as president of the wardroom mess, decreed a Guest Night Dinner. Invitations were sent to all my Wren friends, and all ships' officers had to wear dinner jackets in honour of the occasion. The wardroom stewards laid on a stupendous menu, which I am sure included steak and kidney pie and probably plum duff for pudding – naval favourites – washed down with plenty of pink gins, white ladies, gimlets and dry martinis.

The ritual of dinner concluded with clearing the table and passing the port, after which the loyal toast and many other toasts were made to the newly engaged couple, the captain and his wife, absent wives and girlfriends, the nearest admiral and so on.

After this, traditional high jinks were the order of the day and those who declined to participate wedged themselves securely out of harm's way. First came a game of Wardroom Polo, ridden on chairs with spoons as sticks and one of the remaining potatoes as the ball. After further refreshment all round, the indoor torpedo was fired, with all the appropriate drill recited by the gunner, the missile being the midshipman who was projected the length of the shiny dining room table at the target, which was the settee at the end.

Finally, with everyone well lubricated, the Obstacle Race took place when they all had to circumnavigate the wardroom without touching the deck. This ended with lights out because of the black-out, with the participants having to squeeze through the ship's side scuttle, climb over the top and in again by the other side. This of course made people very thirsty – again.

My fellow Wrens were delighted that John and I had decided to get married. They thoroughly approved of him.

John liked to keep diaries and years later, I read his account of *Oribi*'s sojourn in Belfast and our whirlwind courtship in his unpublished memoir. He wrote:

"In the 14 days it took Harland and Wolfe to patch us up I met and became engaged to Christian Oldham, my wife today. She was then a third officer WRNS in charge of a watch at Maritime Headquarters and was among a party of Wren officers invited to drinks in the wardroom on our first night in harbour – so in true naval style no time was wasted. Her girls – who dubbed themselves 'the Hags watch' – insisted on sending me this reference, stamped SECRET and dated April 12, 1943:

We have pleasure in giving you a reference for Miss Christian Oldham. We have known her for five months, and find her honest, sober, kind and cheerful at all times. In fact, she has never been seen in a temper or known to be bossy. She is quite approachable in the mornings though rather dopey for the first few minutes after waking. There has been a slight tendency to madness during the past fortnight, but otherwise she is considered normal, healthy and cleanly.

Signed Mary Allen, Elizabeth Briggs and Mary Clone."

John continued: "Today, 47 years later I would not fault that analysis except to remark that even if Christian was never bossy with her subordinates in the service she has shown no such scruples to her husband, and has always demonstrated a healthy independence towards senior officers and their ladies but got on very well with the sailors. I put it down to her being a rear-admiral's daughter."

(I might add that if you are landed with three children who all have to be dressed suitably, packed up and unpacked to travel from one naval establishment to another round the world, you do develop a certain amount of bossiness necessary to make everything take off in good naval time which usually means five minutes early!)

I had agreed to marry John knowing very little about him but there was no time now. I would just have to have faith in my own judgment and find out in due course the most exciting stories.

Gradually I came to learn of the calibre of man I had chosen. Like my father, John had joined the navy as a teenager, attending the Royal Naval College at Dartmouth from the age of 13. John's own father too was a navy man, an engineer-captain, but he left the service at 50 to become a vicar in the Church of England. This was something that would raise a few questions when John and I discussed getting married, since my own family was Catholic. Neither of us saw it as a particular obstacle however.

In his own memoir, John described the experience of being accepted to study at Dartmouth with his usual humour.

"The sense of achievement at passing into Dartmouth soon wore off as the screw turned. But it had meant a lot at the time, with only one in 10 of the applicants successful. The written exam was stiffer than the Common Entrance to public schools and an interview had to be passed before you could even sit for that. This interview was the greatest hurdle of all. First came a medical which, as I recall, amounted to an eye test then, after stripping, a vigorous tweaking of the balls was followed by being made to pick up a pencil from the floor by bending the toes. An essay had to be written while waiting for the summons to appear before the Board which was presided over by an admiral, supported by the Captain and the Director of Studies of the College, a public-school headmaster and a senior civil servant representing, presumably, the Commissioners.

"Questions fired at the boy were intended to reveal his personality, acumen, interest in the service to which, if selected, he would be devoting his life; and above all whether, already a gentleman, he would make a good officer and leader. Typical was a well-known *Punch* cartoon of the '20s. 'Can you tell me the names of three famous British Admirals?' demanded an impressive, bewhiskered figure at the head of the table. 'Drake, Nelson, Beatty and I beg your pardon, sir, I didn't catch your name,' the young hopeful replied."

John wrote at length about those formative years at Dartmouth, which were not always very much fun. Of his first day, he said:

"The Term met together for the first time in January 1930, at Paddington Station where we were greeted by our Term Officer, Lieut.-Commander D.C. Hill, a man we came to fear and who I remember hearing say on the telephone to his, presume, wife later as I was about to be beaten, Hang on dear and you'll hear a cadet being whacked!' However, he was all smiles that day, doubtless to impress our parents."

In those days corporal punishment was still very much the method by which children were kept under control and the regime at Dartmouth was no different from other public schools in that respect. It wasn't just the discipline that was harsh. There was little comfort to be had in the living quarters as John also describes. The food sounds particularly awful.

'Memories are hazy of early days at Dartmouth, but I do remember that the first meal was good and gave an unfair impression of culinary delights to be anticipated. I think it was 'seagull' – as chicken was dubbed on its rare appearances. More frequently on offer was a dish we knew as 'beagles' balls', i.e., rissoles…

"Our Gunroom, where we lived and had our being in such spare time as the strict routine allowed, was devoid of any comfort beyond oak benches and tables. The nearest soft seated chairs were in the Reference Library which you only used when a senior college cadet.

"The Term's two dormitories were equally spartan and devoid of heating. They were separated by the Term Officer's cabin and the washrooms, with a convenient lobby for beatings. A weekly hot bath was allowed, with a compulsory cold plunge every morning, I became skilled at the latter by turning out quickly, immersing my head, splashing about a bit and then towelling vigorously before the Cadet Captain noticed.

"Although beds were made for us and shoes cleaned, tidiness was a fetish and sea chests were inspected nightly at rounds when they were lined up at the foot of our iron beds like ranks of guardsmen. Each had a flap that came down, on which your daily gear had to be laid out in a specified order, every item folded in an individual way which, incidentally, I use still when packing. The upper half of the sea chest was separate from the lower, for ease of carriage and stowage and, with the flap down, was open to expose spare shirts, socks, stiff collars and underwear, all in symmetrical piles.

"Slackness covered a multitude of sins and, if personal, was rewarded with punishment marks which added up to a beating. For general slackness the whole term was awarded a 'strafe,' which could take a variety of forms. Those most common entailed everybody turning in 30 minutes early. When the whistle blew you changed (known as 'shifted') into sports gear, doubled down those awful steps to Sandquay and back, then got into Number One uniform, stiff collar and all, and fell in for inspection with everything stowed away. Good for the soul, I suppose, but hard on the buttons, and it certainly taught you to change your clothes quickly, which often came in useful.

"Each working day, after early prep and breakfast, there was drill on the parade ground, using ancient and enormous rifles of at least Boer War vintage. As the lowest of the low, we were also taught how to salute and who, which included all officers and masters and the Quarter Deck. This was the great central, indoor place of assembly, decorated with silk ensigns, statues of royal sailors (there have been plenty) and historic uniforms in glass cases, beautiful sailing-ship models and other naval memorabilia.

"Here Evening Quarters were held, and Divisions (prayers) if wet. Once a week, after evening prep, cadets were taught to dance

– an essential accomplishment in those flag-showing days when there was still lots of red on the maps, marking the British Empire. It was strictly fox-trot and waltz to the sedate accompaniment of a Royal Marine pensioner orchestra. Cadets partnered each other, taking turns to be girl and this was so traditional as not to be considered the least unusual. It was deemed a great honour if the Term Officer or a cadet captain invited ('told' is perhaps the better word) you to dance with him, and there was no question as to who led. Nobody mixed outside his own term and it all seemed very pure then, but just imagine what the papers would say today."

John concluded:

"Although my time at Dartmouth was not enjoyable I have not the slightest doubt that it did me a great deal of good; in fact, it moulded a boy who started wet behind the ears into a reasonable sort of man. Even if the wings of some were clipped – especially those with high academic or artistic gifts – the system produced a pretty good average that more than proved its worth in two world wars and paid a heavy price. A quarter of my Term lost their lives.

"And the spartan style of living together with the strictest of discipline must have been the right introduction to the Service for young men destined to command and care for sailors in good times and bad. There is a story of a Captain RN, survivor of the Java Sea Battle who, when released from the Japanese in 1945, was asked how he had got on. 'If you can survive Dartmouth, you can survive anything,' reputedly was his reply."

A GLIMPSE OF NAZI GERMANY

Thus, John survived Dartmouth and in 1934 he went to sea on HMS *Frobisher*, the college's training ship, as a 'snotty', which was the naval term for a midshipman, an officer of the lowest rank. The name derives from the fact that the snotties' uniforms were made without pockets in which to stow a handkerchief and their jackets had three buttons at the cuffs to prevent them from using their sleeves instead.

In 1936, John gained his first gold stripe, becoming a sub-lieutenant on HMS *Neptune*, a newly built Leander-class light cruiser. It was on this ship that he would have his first encounter with the Kriegsmarine, the navy of Nazi Germany. The name 'Kriegsmarine', with which Hitler had replaced the 'Reichsmarine' (Realm Navy), meant 'the War Navy', which perhaps should have given some warning of his frame of mind.

It was the year of the Berlin Olympics and *Neptune* had been chosen to represent Great Britain and the Royal Navy at Germany's famous Kiel Week, which would that year include the Olympic regatta. Kiel Week, or the Kieler Hoche, as it was properly known, began as a sort of competition between Kaiser Wilhelm II and his English cousin, King George V, as they vied to build the biggest yachts and the best battleships in Europe. Now Hitler saw it as an important event at which to display the sea-going might of the Third Reich.

Neptune's presence was seen as a goodwill gesture to mark the Anglo-German Naval Agreement which had legalised the Kriegsmarine's hitherto covert rearmament. John would later say of that treaty:

"As professionals, those of us who gave any thought to the matter were mostly glad that a greatly respected fellow sea service had had its honour restored, and I am not ashamed to admit that throughout the war I still thought of the German Navy as fellow professionals doing the same sort of job as me, only on the other side. But, of course, there was no naval SS."

Indeed, many German naval officers privately abhorred the Nazi regime and in 1936, John could not have imagined that within three years the men of the Kriegsmarine would become his deadly enemies. He was simply looking forward to the chance to take part in one of the world's biggest regattas and see the Germans' most famous ships up close. This opportunity to inspect new ships, such as the 'pocket battleship', the *Graf Spee*, would provide the Royal Navy with valuable intelligence, and John was among those sent to survey the Kriegsmarine's vessels.

John describes the event:

"En route, we went through the Kiel Canal, which was a great experience. The waterway twists and turns amidst lush pasture land and it seemed hardly possible that an ocean-going ship could penetrate into such depths of country, while at bends the masts and funnels of some other vessel would stick up from the middle of a cluster of farm buildings in a most surprising way.

'This was our introduction to Germany, and right from the start we were greeted from the banks and cheered on our way. But nowhere was *Neptune's* progress welcomed more enthusiastically than at a girls' school about half way, where a young lady waved a Union Jack with such frenzy that she almost fell in. I wonder who she was and what the future held for her, this British schoolgirl who became noted for the greeting she never failed to give to all Royal Navy ships that passed that way in the mid-thirties.

"Kiel was colourful and gay with ships and yachts of many nations dressed overall with bunting, and the prominent Nazi swastikas were then more of a novelty than a menace. By contrast, over on the dockyard side, the covered shipbuilding slips where it was rumoured U-boats were under construction, were a hive of activity. That was the sight as *Neptune* entered Kiel Bay with band playing, guard paraded, ship's company lining the decks, and the time-honoured naval ceremonial was enacted in turn as each foreign warship was passed. There were the billows of smoke and reverberating thuds of gun salutes, with bugle calls, the shrilling of bosuns' pipes and the strains of national anthems, each navy trying to outshine the others.

"Immediately on anchoring, a German boat came alongside, crew faultless with their boat-hook drill, pendant flying to indicate the officer of the guard was onboard, and on this as on many other occasions we were struck by the similarity in appearance and ceremonial between the German Navy and our own. We were berthed close to the pocket battleship *Graf Spee* and our interest in her as a new class about which the Admiralty wanted to know a lot more, would have been intensified had we but known that in a few years our sister ship *Ajax* would be in action against her on the other side of the world.

"As assistant to *Neptune's* intelligence officer I was involved in efforts to satisfy the Director of Naval Intelligence's curiosity, my particular task being to determine the distance apart of the 11-inch guns in the new-fangled triple turrets. I spent hours on our bridge taking sextant angles and ranges, getting a different answer each time. However, I was able eventually to pace it out easily during a reception on *Graf Spee's* quarter-deck!

"The Germans were admirable hosts and invitations came thick and fast, more than could be fitted in comfortably between ship and regatta duties. Over drinks in wardroom and gunroom, our opposite numbers, while consuming vast quantities of neat Scotch, would invariably tax us with the same subject: the logic of friendship between Germany and Great Britain as opposed to their own new alliance with despised Italy. 'Can't you see how much more we have in common with you than with the Italians?' our new friends argued. 'It's ridiculous that your allies should be your old enemies, the French. We Anglo-Saxons ought to be uniting against the threat of Bolshevism,' and so on, in the same theme.

But there was a competitive edge to the hospitality too, as John describes:

"Apart from the Olympic Regatta there was an international naval athletics meeting for which our teams were duly landed, although with no great confidence in the outcome. The discomfort of *Neptune's* sailors was complete when they found themselves first on parade to march round the stadium in best Olympic style. Orders were given in German, which they could not understand and resented on principle, and British tooth-sucking could be felt if not heard during a lengthy and incomprehensible harangue by the port admiral. It was about then that we began to suspect that the German Navy's ways were not, after all, ours, and *Neptune's* team was greatly consoled before the day was out when the Italians out-pulled the Herrenvolk (the master race) in that essentially masculine contest, the tug-of-war!"

After the Regatta, John and a number of members of *Neptune's* crew were taken to the Olympic Games in Berlin as official guests. They were flown there in a Fokker bomber. John's account of the trip gives an insight into the Games that Hitler intended to use to showcase the power of Nazi Germany. He describes the vast stadium, built to accommodate 100,000, like a Roman amphitheatre, with stone seats that were "excruciatingly uncomfortable". A processional flight of 150 steps was designed to make the arrival of VIPs more impressive. John saw some of Germany's biggest dignitaries during his visit, including Adolf Hitler himself.

"...the Fuhrer arrived at speed in the middle of an enormously impressive cavalcade of black Mercedes open touring cars. After inspecting a military guard-of-honour he proceeded to harangue the crowd for what seemed a very long time but clearly not too long for his German audience judging by the bursts of applause and successions of responsive 'Heils'. We just minded our own business, earning in the process some dirty looks as our arms were not raised in salute. However, we were in good company in our gesture, which was shared by two fellow guests of my own age sitting next to us: they, in intriguing juxtaposition, were Prince Frederick of Prussia and the 2nd Earl Jellicoe."

Hitler had planned that the Olympics would demonstrate his ideals of racial supremacy. Prior to the Games, the *Völkischer Beobachter*, the Nazi party's official newspaper, vehemently expressed the view that Jewish and black people should not be allowed to compete. It took the threat of a boycott by other nations including the United States to make Hitler relent and allow them to participate; however, Hitler's displeasure as his Aryan athletes lost time and again to black athletes such as Jesse Owens was clear.

The Berlin authorities had done their best to disguise the racism of the Reich by cleaning up anti-Semitic graffiti in the run up to the Games and by adding a single token Jewish athlete to the German team, but John was not fooled. He describes his sense of growing unease as the crew of the *Neptune* got to know the locals.

"A chance meeting with a Jewish professor, who kindly entertained me at his home, afforded me a glimpse into the future. Despite the apparent happiness of family and professional life, his foreboding at the rising tide of Nazism and the mounting tension could not be disguised. Most people, however, had no such misgivings judging by the dagger looks of the crowd as I, in plain clothes, lifted hat rather than arm when the Horst Wessel song was played at some ceremony or other.

"By the time we were due to leave I think little doubt remained in our minds that Great Britain and Germany were on a collision course. The apparent inevitability of conflict was not made more palatable by the friendliness of our naval hosts, who gave us a rousing send-off at the entrance to the Kiel Canal. There we found a marine band to play us through the lock with airs from Gilbert and Sullivan which, with typical Teutonic thoroughness as well as good manners, they had ascertained was the captain's favourite music.

"At least one good thing for the Royal Navy came out of it all, but much later after so many lives had been lost: the German naval yachts, which we had greatly admired, were transferred to us as reparations in 1945–6. They were christened officially as 'windfalls', which they were indeed, for these boats formed the nucleus of what became eventually a substantial fleet of adventure training craft. They were certainly earned the hard way."

As for *Neptune*, after she returned to Portsmouth, John would never see her again. He was sent to Hong Kong as a sub-lieutenant on the destroyer HMS *Delight*. He spent two years in Hong Kong, before he was called back to Britain as hostilities began in the Atlantic. *Neptune* was eventually mined and sunk off Cap Bon in the last year of the war. John had the job of sweeping the area afterwards when he was commanding a minesweeper.

JOHN'S WAR

Upon his return from Hong Kong, John became first lieutenant of HMS *Vanoc*, a destroyer that had seen service in World War One. He describes her as "so dated that she even carried cutlasses for boarding purposes".

With *Vanoc*, John escorted convoys from Liverpool, until in April 1940, she and other destroyers were ordered north to Scapa Flow, where an expeditionary force was being assembled to counter the German invasion of Norway. *Vanoc* sailed with nine liners loaded with troops to Namsos near Narvik, 120 miles south of the Arctic Circle. This was to be the first occasion on which John came under fire. It wasn't long before the position of the allies in Norway became untenable and in late May an evacuation was ordered, with *Vanoc* having to bring home the troops she had so recently dropped off.

Everywhere, the Allies were in retreat. From Narvik *Vanoc* was despatched straight to France, where the Dunkirk evacuations were underway. At St Nazaire, John witnessed the sinking of the troopship *Lancastria*, "a terrible sight and a great shock" that stayed with him as *Vanoc* escorted a convoy back to Plymouth.

There followed a period of duty in the English Channel before John was transferred to HMS *Glasgow* and sent to the Mediterranean.

By the time I met him in 1943, John was already a decorated naval officer. He had a DSC, the Distinguished Service Cross, awarded for meritorious service before the enemy. During our whirlwind courtship, I came to know how John had been chosen for such an honour. We go back to December 1940 when HMS *Glasgow* was towed into dry dock in Alexandria, having been hit by two aerial torpedoes off Crete. While *Glasgow* underwent repairs, John was sent to Sidi Barrani, on Egypt's Mediterranean coast.

Sidi Barrani saw fierce fighting in December 1940, at the beginning of Operation Compass, as the Allies took back the town from the Italian Army. It was all but over by 12 December, with the Italians having retreated back to Sollum, now called Salûm, a village close to the Libyan border. This was the situation when John was sent ashore to support the British Army who were stocking up with supplies and evacuating Italian prisoners.

John wrote in his memoirs:

"I was to be beachmaster and within hours I was sailing westwards with my three sailors in a naval auxiliary vessel. As darkness fell we transferred to lighter X39, a relic of the 1915 Dardanelles, which meanwhile had arrived with supplies for the military. Sollum had not been taken as reported so we headed for land nearer Sidi Barrani.

"As our clumsy X39 craft approached land and began to wallow in the ground swell, figures appeared in both khaki and blue grey

Italian to greet us. Soon several hundred prisoners had formed a chain and were busy unloading fuel, water and provisions and looked happy at having something to do. Having got this organised I set off to report to the local army HQ some way in land, reached by a track that crossed the debris of the previous day's battle for Sidi Barrani, the first military British success of WW2; guns, rifles, wrecked vehicles, burned out tanks and bodies, still lying where they had fallen. Soon my guide drew up alongside an inconspicuous hummock in the sand; in reply to his 'Hulloa,' a military head rose neck-high, like the Jinn of the magic lamp and beckoned me down into an ancient Egyptian tomb, where a brigadier and his staff were working in this ready-made bomb-proof shelter, which was their HQ. They were most surprised to see a sailor!

"After a briefing I returned to the beach where I found my chaps had requisitioned the former enemy postal tent as a mess and established a signal station and prudently dug a slit trench. Next day we suffered the first of many sand storms, accompanied by heavy rain and thunder, reducing visibility to less than a hundred yards and penetrating one's person, clothes, tent, food, everything; anti-gas goggles saved the eyes. Meanwhile, so far as the storm permitted, more prisoners were being brought in until an estimated 10,000 were assembled in a rudimentary cage, almost unguarded as they had lost all fight, and anyway there was nowhere for them to go. Italian medics attended to their needs.

"We broke camp that afternoon and set off for Sollum with me at the wheel of a captured lorry in company with an RASC convoy, a boat's ensign flying proudly at a mast we had fixed to the cab. The main coastal road had been built by the Italians, but never finished, and was deeply furrowed, with the added complication of frequent bomb craters which were my undoing on several occasions. Fortunately there was no shortage of other vehicles to tow us out. Darkness came halfway through our journey and we halted at Buq Buq, camping under the lorry. The convoy got underway early next morning but I lost my leader in the confusion of an infantry brigade also moving forward. Under the impression that he had got ahead, I pressed on, overtaking vehicle after vehicle until, to my consternation I found that we appeared to be leading the entire British Army. We kept on and soon reached a village which was a complete wreck; there was a hovel near the harbour pier which at least had the distinction of having a roof, and this we appropriated, hoisting the White Ensign and inscribing Admiralty House on the door. Thus, I became Naval-Officer-In-Charge Sollum.

"The unloading of supply ships began immediately with prisoner labour encouraged by the remnants of a company of the Argyll and Sutherland Highlanders, who had been left behind to picket the place while the rest of the Desert Highland Force advanced towards Bardia. Their commander, a bizarre figure, kitted out in an Italian brigadier's tunic topped by his regimental Glengarry, since most of his own uniform was no longer fit to wear, dubbed himself 'King's Harbour Master' and was of enormous help. Eventually we were bringing in almost 500 tons daily in lighters manned by a fine crowd of New Zealand sappers who suffered casualties from mines and bombs. Each night RASC convoys drove out into the desert, steering by compass to drop supply dumps behind the enemy for our advancing 7th Armoured Division.

'Of course, the enemy did not leave us alone to get on with it. Our only fighters were the nimble but outdated Gladiators who engaged in many spectacular 'Biggles' type dog-fights with not dissimilar biplane CR42s. Our worst attack came on Christmas Eve when 12 Italian bombers were suddenly right above us in the clear blue sky. The work of unloading lighters was in full swing at the jetties, when a split-second later, whistles of bombs filled the air. There were five direct hits on the jetty and craft, leaving 25 dead or dying all around me.

"When work was resumed it was found that 500 of the recently arrived Cypriot labourers had fled to the hills, leaving still more work for the New Zealanders who had been the worst hit.

"General O'Connor visited us several times to see how we were getting on – he exuded confidence and always seemed complete master of the situation. The XIII Corps conference prior to the attack on Bardia was held in 'Admiralty House' and was a most unusual experience for a sailor like me. At other times we also saw Admiral Andrew Cunningham and Generals Wavell and Jumbo Wilson.

"My next job was an odd one; acting as a lighthouse for the 2nd Battle Squadron (BS), when it made a landfall prior to carrying out an early bombardment north of the Bardia-Tobruk road, which immediately preceded the assault on Bardia.

"The army drove me some distance to an outpost held by the Durham Light Infantry where, after a very civilised dinner in the mess tent, I was turned out into the dark and lonely desert, pointed in the right direction and told to keep walking by compass course for 60 minutes which would bring me to high ground overlooking the sea. Sometime after midnight – I have forgotten the exact hour – I was to flash a prearranged signal with my Aldis lamp on a certain seaward bearing and keep this up for 20 minutes, after which I was free to go home. Apparently this would provide the flagship with a point of departure for the run-in to the bombardment position.

"It was eerie up there on the escarpment by myself, pondering where the nearest enemy were and no glint of acknowledgement from the great darkened battleships. For years I wondered whether it had all been a ghastly failure until, much later, I found out quite by chance that all had gone to plan. Well after the war I happened to be lunching at a Service club in Pall Mall with my father-in-law and was introduced to a retired admiral friend who, I recalled, had been in command of the 2nd BS at the time. 'Please do tell me,' I ventured to ask the great man, 'was the light I flashed from the desert when you were on your way to bombard Bardia before dawn on January 3 1941 in the proper place and at the correct time?' He looked rather surprised at being taken back so many years. 'Oh, so that was you,' he replied. 'I did wonder who was behind that glimmer of light in the blackness. Yes it was fine.' My sigh of relief must have been audible to both admirals."

The Battle of Bardia went well – it was the first battle of the war predominantly fought by Australians on the Allied side – and soon the Allies were able to push on into Libya, forcing the Italians into retreat. It was for his part in enabling the successful bombardment that John was awarded the DSC "For courage, skill and devotion to duty off the Libyan coast".

THE IMPORTANCE
OF WEATHER

After his adventure in North Africa, John returned to HMS *Glasgow* and stayed with her for another year. She was sent first to Singapore, where her bow and stern could be strengthened. *Glasgow* stayed in Singapore until the end of 1941, and though the threat of war loomed large, John found that "civilian life continued as usual… offices closed every afternoon for several hours, clubs and hotels were packed each midday for tiffin and again in the evening for sundowners like stenghas and gin-slings, and there was an endless round of parties."

Just a couple of months later, the Japanese invaded and thousands of Allied troops and British ex-pats were made prisoners of war.

After spending time in the Indian Ocean and the United States, John returned to Britain to become first lieutenant of HMS *Oribi*, a new fleet destroyer. His time with her was to be rather less congenial than his last tour with the *Glasgow*. *Oribi* was first sent to the Arctic. John wrote:

"My eighteen months in her coincided with a very tough, if not the toughest period of the war at sea, which included not only the apogee of the Battle of the Atlantic but also the passage of seven convoys to Russia and the return of survivors. These shiploads of vitally needed war supplies for the Soviet forces were fought through by the Allies in the face of the worst possible weather and within easy range of German air, surface and underwater attack for three quarters of their 2,000-mile journey. *Oribi* was also involved in a couple of operations to relieve Spitzbergen at latitude 78N in the Arctic Ocean; the first trip, in winter was uneventful except for the weather, but the second, in the permanent daylight of summer, was a very different matter. In all we earned seven endorsements to our Blue Nose certificates.

"If you ask a Russian convoy veteran what he remembers most about them he will probably recall the terrible weather just as vividly as enemy action. It was rarely safe to venture on deck where you were either liable to get washed over the side or slip overboard into Arctic waters. We sprayed exposed working areas with scalding water led from the boiler room, but this froze on impact and only made things worse. Meanwhile rigging and guard-rails grew as thick as a man's arm; picks and hammers were the only answer. The ship's stability would be jeopardised and when she rolled, she would often hover at the point of no return before deciding to right herself, decks awash and the sea sometimes even lapping the wings of the lower bridge. It was very alarming – much worse than the enemy!

"Sea conditions permitting, guns and torpedo tubes were kept operable with electric heating coils fitted to blank cartridges in their breeches, while muzzles were covered by the sailors' universal friend – French letters!"

Oribi was next ordered to join the 3rd Support Group of fleet destroyers to form a fast mobile defence force that could dash from one convoy to another and be refuelled at sea. Her first encounter as part of this force was in defence of convoy HX-230 in a terrible gale. Five U-boats were on the attack but were driven off with the loss of just one merchant ship. Having headed off that danger, *Oribi* was quickly despatched to help defend a convoy of 57 ships which was being tailed by seven U-boats.

John describes how they were able to move with such speed and efficiency:

"We had a brilliant new secret piece of equipment which at this stage of the war proved its worth... The High Frequency Direction Finding picked up a strong transmission which its operator identified as a U-boat meteorological report. In less than an hour it had been confirmed by the Admiralty, (this would have been the work of Wrens at Bletchley Park) fixing the position within 20 miles of us; at full speed ahead we soon sighted two U-boats on the surface recharging their batteries; after dropping a pattern of depth charges we hurried back to protect the convoy."

It was during one of these actions that *Oribi* picked up "an oily solitary figure clinging to a small piece of wreckage", who turned out to be the captain of a U-boat, a korvettankapitan. Though the weather made it difficult, he was fished out of the sea, at considerable risk to the sailors who had to go over the side to fix a line to him. The sole survivor, he was badly wounded, with a great gash the whole length of one arm. He was brought onboard and taken to the wardroom, which was transformed into an operating theatre. John describes the efforts to which the *Oribi's* crew went to save the German captain's arm:

"Our young medical officer, Surgeon Lieutenant John Smith, a Glasgow gynaecologist in civilian life, operated on him. The lively motion of the ship, travelling at some speed, necessitated lashing the patient to the dining room table whose polished top was covered in a tarpaulin; the surgeon was strapped to the deck support stanchion with a sailor to steady him; to his left the sick berth attendant was wedged holding the instruments, and from the other side a wardroom steward stood by to mop his brow. He made a superb job of putting in 30 or 40 of the neatest stitches from wrist to armpit – as neat as any he might have made."

All the while, the ship continued to pitch and roll, water washed around the mess decks while the upper deck was out of bounds. The equinoctial gales, into which they had steamed at high speed, had caused *Oribi* serious structural damage. A crack had been discovered, extending a third of the way across what was known as the 'iron deck', a toughened steel deck amidships, over the engine room, to which the two quadruple torpedo tubes were secured. Left unrepaired, such damage could lead to a 'broken back', hence *Oribi* was detached forthwith to the nearest port which, as fate decreed, happened to be Belfast, where I was working in the plotting room, quite unaware that romance was sailing in my direction.

Two weeks and a marriage proposal later, *Oribi* was ready to sail again.

It was lucky for us that Hitler had refused to heed the sound advice of his u-boat chief Admiral Dönitz, which was to double the number of U-boats and concentrate them on the North Atlantic, blowing up as many of our desperately needed tankers and supply ships on their way to and from England as possible. Hitler liked to think he could command the seas by keeping all his great battleships, such as the *Tirpitz* and *Bismarck*, in reserve like huge white elephants. The real reason was that we were more than a match for them. Thus, while they lurked in port, we built convoy escorts as quickly as possible. But now Hitler had realised his naval chief was right, and the Germans were turning out over 70 of their deadly U-boats every quarter; by May 1943 it was estimated that 143 were lying in wait for our convoys. This was probably the climax of the North Atlantic battle and into all this mayhem sailed the 3rd Support Group.

HMS *Oribi* left Belfast on 29 April to re-join the Group that had been ordered to reinforce the escort of ONS-5, a slow convoy of 43 ships bound for North America. As I bid farewell to my new fiancé, I could not have imagined what would happen next.

ORIBI UNDER ATTACK

After my whirlwind romance and engagement, it was back to work in the plotting room. It was business as usual, though now for the first time I had a special interest in plotting a particular convoy. As ONS-5 began to move slowly across the Atlantic, I followed her progress on the wall map with close attention.

The weather in the Atlantic that spring was not ideal for making the crossing, which had to go far to the north, and about a week after leaving Belfast, the convoy hit a storm. As it fought its way through mountainous seas and hurricane-force winds, its speed was reduced to one knot. Worse was to come as four U-boats were known to be in contact, with many more shadowing the armada.

John recounts in his memoirs:

"By May 1st the weather had worsened so much that the ships were virtually stopped and losing formation. In his report, Commander P.W. Gretton, escort force commander, wrote that it was 'blowing like the bells of hell.'

"Next day a temporary lull found the convoy scattered over 30 miles among ice flows and growlers, but the ships were successfully rounded up just in time for another gale that evening. Thirteen more U-boats joined the attack on May 3, with many more threatening; 24 hours later with the convoy still crawling into the teeth of the gale, Dönitz ordered 27 boats to form a new patrol line… On May 5, 40 U-boats were directed against ONS-5…"

Back at Belfast Castle, from the first report of the impending battle over ONS-5, the plot where I was on watch became the focus of attention. Signal after signal came in and the teleprinter buzzed on relentlessly. Waiting for news became unbearable and no one wanted to go off duty. The build-up was slow to start with and of course we did not realise what a drama it was to be.

The tension grew as *Oribi* was obviously headed straight for the 'wolf pack' and the plot in front of us became a vivid picture of the action, with all of us taking a vicarious part in it.

My plotters tried with various spurious excuses to persuade me to change watch so I might not know of the highly dangerous drama evolving. But of course I could not possibly leave the scene. I had to be able to see what was happening. I knew that if I was not in the plotting room, hearing the news as it came in, I would not be able to put it out of my mind. I wouldn't be able to sleep or rest. I would only be able to wonder what was going on and assume the very worst. It was better for me to be there in the thick of it. I knew I was experiencing just a fraction of the fear that John and his crew must be facing. But having just secured this man, I was truly worried that I might now lose him.

Our hopes were briefly raised as a Royal Canadian Air Force Catalina sank one of the U-boats and damaged another.

John picks up the story:

"Apart from the 3rd Support Group there were four Flower-class corvettes acting as escorts of the convoy: *Sunflower, Snowflake, Loosestrife* and *Pink*, as well as *Tay* and *Vidette*, and another fleet destroyer *Offa*. The battle raged: six U-boats sank seven of the convoy ships, *Vidette* damaged U 270, while *Oribi* and *Offa* attacking in succession drove three more U-boats off. Another three were damaged by other escorts with HMS *Pink* protecting the stragglers 30 miles astern. The following day as many as 19 U-boats were in contact, and *Tay* actually sighted seven on the surface at one time charging batteries, and of these U 638 was sunk by *Loosestrife*. In the small hours of May 6 we located U 531 by radar and forced her to dive before she was sunk. Minutes later we rammed U 125 which was then finished off by *Vidette*."

John goes on:

"Earlier that night I had been keeping the First Watch during which the explosions as four ships were torpedoed in quick succession were felt rather than heard and, as I recall, we commented 'poor devils.' By midnight the weather had turned to mist and things had quietened down, so 'defence stations' was piped, which meant that only 50% of the armament was manned, allowing half of the people to get some much-needed rest. I turned in fully clothed in the sick-bay below the bridge, which I used if a cot was vacant, as this avoided the longish and potentially dangerous trip along the exposed upper deck to my cabin.

"I was abruptly awakened by a terrific crash and bump. My first thought was that we had been torpedoed, then that the ship had gone aground as we seemed to ride up over something, but I soon realised that was not possible since the nearest land was miles away. These thoughts flashed through my head as I scrambled out of the cot but I was unable to find the deck; instead my feet were floundering on bottles and other glass objects and I found that I was trying to get on the bulkhead, or wall side, which was then more horizontal than the deck as we had heeled over so far. On this, normally vertical, surface were racks of medicine bottles and sick-bay utensils on which I was attempting to stand. Of course, all this only took seconds and by the time the alarm gongs began clanging I had scaled the two flights of ladder to the bridge. There I followed the eyes of the watch-keepers and saw a conning-tower close alongside and below us to port, realising it was a U-boat. I do recall not saying 'poor devils' on that occasion.

"From the bridge I watched incredulously as the ship tried to ride over the submarine we had rammed and whose conning tower was clinging crazily to our portside. We were in the very centre of the action and all around, occasionally lit up by a star shell, were corvettes attacking deadly and daring U-boats, still on the surface, who in turn were trying to get a few more of the convoy before they had to dive. Every now and again would come a 'crump', another explosion and in the background, the incessant 'ping, ping, ping' of the ASDIC, with frequent 'ping go' as it picked up its target, like theme music in a nightmare film…"

In the plotting room, I too felt as though I was in that nightmare film, knowing that each signal that came in was already a couple of minutes out of date and that in the time it had taken to reach the plot, anything might have happened. I would not be able to tear myself away from the plot until I knew that *Oribi* was safe again. Though I tried to maintain a calm exterior, on the inside I was racked with anxiety.

I do not know how I managed to get through those fraught days while ONS-5 and *Oribi*, in whose wardroom I had so recently celebrated my engagement to the man I loved, was under attack. Each hour seemed to last an eternity, until at last the Royal Canadian Air Force was within range and the residue of the bitterly defended convoy sailed safely on to its destination.

Of course the story of the U-boat attack on ONS-5 was widely reported in the British papers. I kept all the press cuttings I could gather to show John upon his return. Among them was a cutting from the *Daily Express*. Under the headline "WAR'S BIGGEST U-BATTLE: Navy beats off 25," the incident was reported thus:

> *Escort ships of the Royal Navy with aircraft of the Royal Canadian Air Force, have successfully defended a west-bound Atlantic convoy against a series of determined and sustained attacks by a powerful force of U-boats. The attacks and counter-attacks extended intermittently for eight days and nights.*

When the figures were verified, it was declared that out of the convoy of 43 ships, 12 had been lost, but of the 40 U-boats involved, eight were destroyed and 12 damaged, including a U-boat carrying what was described as "a new secret weapon". This victory for the Allies had repercussions. It is recorded that a furious Hitler ordered a decommissioning of all heavy ships in favour of concentrating on the U-boat arm of the navy. Admiral Raeder was forced to resign and was succeeded by Dönitz, chief of the submarine service and master of the wolf pack. But even Dönitz was running scared after losing so many of his fleet in such a short period of time. The German submariners reportedly dubbed that month 'Black May'.

The failed attack on ONS-5 was a turning point for the Germans. Dönitz decided that wolf pack activities would have to be suspended pending an increase in the number of U-boats. The Kriegsmarine had lost the advantage. The efforts of the Allied navies combined with an increase in air cover had all but eliminated the notorious Atlantic Gap. Meanwhile, the introduction of the Leigh Light, a powerful search light fitted to the RAF's Coastal Command bombers, meant that U-boats were easier to find and destroy when they disappeared off radar. With the enemy thus hampered, the North Atlantic convoys were able to bring more men and materials from North America in preparation for the second front.

Once she was out of danger from the U-boats, the damage to *Oribi* was assessed. Thankfully she was still watertight. Only the fore-peak and lower central floor were flooded. Her ASDIC gear was still intact (ASDIC was the name of the sonar equipment on our ships). Once *Oribi's* crew had shored up her bow, she resumed her station until she was detached to make for St John's in Newfoundland, Canada. At 12 knots, which was her maximum safe speed, it took almost three days for her to get there. Once in dry dock at St John's, *Oribi's* bow was reinforced with concrete, before she sailed down to Boston in the USA, where more permanent repairs were carried out.

While *Oribi* was in Newfoundland, John and I were able to be in contact again, which was a big relief. We celebrated *Oribi's* deliverance and the skill of John and the rest of her valiant crew.

My mother could start planning our wedding.

CLAIRVOYANT CATS

It was about this time that my sister Anne came to visit me in Belfast. Having first trained as a nurse at the Longmore Hospital in Edinburgh, she had joined the WAAF, the Women's Auxiliary Air Force. She was a linguist and with her fluent French and German she was a valuable member of the service – a sergeant, no less. Her job included listening in to German conversations among aircraft crew which might be valuable intelligence information. She was stationed on the east coast near Lincoln, not far from Europe where this sort of communication went on. She must have had some leave when she came to visit me and this was quite a problem living as I did in the officers' mess. However, her interesting occupation must have disguised her being only a sergeant, which I thought was pretty grand anyway.

Anne was always getting engaged to young men, and then finding one she liked better, so had come over to Belfast to help me get ready for my wedding – and perhaps to make sure I was doing the right thing, having heard the saga of my getting engaged to John after only knowing him for 10 days! I so enjoyed having her there; we were very close friends, always, and during the war communications were so difficult; you had to make an appointment even for a telephone call and these were very inadequate. It was much better to see Anne in person.

It would be a while before I was able to see John again, though in the autumn of 1943, he was back in Northern Ireland with *Oribi* for a training exercise.

Although the Admiralty boffins had recently come up with the new secret High Frequency Direction Finder of which John spoke, which had been found extremely valuable when dealing with U-boats, Hitler had come up with a new threat. As well as the magnetic and acoustic mines, he now had the 'Gnat', a magnetic and acoustic torpedo, which was also electric homing. *Oribi* was sent to the Escort Forces Base at Londonderry to practise counter measures against this new German weapon. Here, the Third Support Group was joined by a Polish ship called the ORP *Orkan*. She was an M-class destroyer, whose name translated as *Windstorm*.

The ships were just ready to sail when there was a hail from the bridge of the Polish ship: "Our cats have disappeared – have you got them?"

Sailors are very superstitious and this was a serious matter. As it happened, three cats had been spotted joining *Oribi* moments before, so several of *Orkan*'s sailors were sent to retrieve them. It was not an easy task. The cats protested vehemently. With not a little difficulty, the Polish sailors managed to recapture two of their cats but the third, with a violent shriek and a flash of claw, escaped and hid under one of *Oribi*'s gun platforms, where she was allowed to remain.

The ships set sail, but a few days later *Oribi* and *Orkan* found themselves alongside one another again as they stopped to refuel from a tanker lying off Moville in Donegal. It wasn't long before one of *Orkan*'s cats was discovered to have made a break for *Oribi* again, escaping via the tanker. A signal was sent from *Oribi* to *Orkan* and a small boat was despatched to bring the escapee back. Later that day, *Oribi's* original stowaway was coaxed out from beneath the gun platform and was seen to be pure black in colour. The shade of the cat's coat was taken as a particularly good omen for *Oribi*, which she had now made her home.

Before sailing, any ship destined for time at sea would be visited by boats from the Irish Republic side of the river, laden with eggs, butter, bacon and other items which found ready buyers. This commerce would be duly noted by enemy agents based on the Republic bank who would also report to their masters the ships' sailing times and last known course.

John continues the story at Moville:

"A few nights later, the destroyers were stationed in line abreast, carrying out a sweep towards a reported U-boat position – I had the Middle Watch and was about to take a sip from a mug of steaming hot cocoa – when there was a distant explosion; in the corner of the bridge the muffled-up radio operator, crouched over his tiny blue light, took down a message as it came in. Immediately everyone came to Action Stations, with the Captain already up, summoned by voice pipe from his sea cabin and strident alarm gongs, which roused the watch below. The signal was from *Orkan* reporting the explosion close astern – this signal was to be her last. The very next minute our ASDIC picked up a hydrophone effect from the torpedo – the Gnat – which on its way to *Orkan* passed close to and narrowly missed our screws, the beat of which would have set it off – then almost simultaneously, our Polish consort, next in line and less than a mile away, suddenly became a terrible red glow from end to end – she had ignited, her steel hull turned to transparent red glass, revealing violent blazing furnaces below – then the thunderous explosion stunned our horrified ears. As the shattering sound died away, the surrounding sea and sky blazed with incandescent fragments fluttering down – a deathly stillness hung about the night. Instantaneously a vast ship, a living pulsating entity, a destroyer identical to our own, had vanished, leaving a ghostly gap, her 200 brave men consigned to oblivion, together with her two clairvoyant cats."

The third clairvoyant cat, which had successfully jumped ship in Londonderry, became *Oribi's* much venerated mascot, closely guarded and pampered by every member of the crew. Panic broke out when she once disappeared for several days. It was only when she returned with six matching black kittens that calm was restored and the fleet was once more able to carry out its naval duties.

My sister Anne's post-war career would touch on this sort of other-worldly happening. Having left the WAAF, she travelled to Italy with the Malcolm Clubs, which were welfare clubs for RAF personnel. It was while she was in Italy that Anne became interested in broadcasting, taking a role as a British Forces Network announcer. The experience led her to join the BBC as a radio journalist in 1948 and she quickly rose to become a distinguished television producer.

Among those programmes Anne produced was a series of documentaries and dramatic re-enactments called *Leap In the Dark*, which investigated claims of telepathy, hauntings, poltergeist activity and psychokinesis (the ability to move objects using only mind power). Anne's programmes were always very well-researched but they were also very entertaining. She was good at getting the best out of her subjects.

Anne's professional stance was that of a sceptic but perhaps that wasn't entirely representative of her views on the supernatural. Among her collaborators was Colin Wise, an author and specialist in ESP (extra-sensory perception), who wrote, "Anne Owen has told me that she had been through a period when she could predict the future. Before a concert with a celebrated cellist, she had a premonition that he would break a string and asked the producer what they should do if this happened; he dismissed it as unlikely. But the string broke eight minutes before the end of the concert."

When he heard that Anne had predicted the string snapping, the cellist refused to speak to her, believing she had somehow caused the string to break.

Perhaps Anne would have understood the Polish cats' feline farsightedness? Was the acoustic attraction some sort of long purr that cats could recognise? Had the cats been indoctrinated by Germans before joining the *Orkan*? Should the navy have investigated? We shall never know!

WRENS CAN DO ANYTHING

As the war continued, the Admiralty found they could depend more and more on the Wrens; recruiting accelerated and we were invited to take part in some of the most specialised jobs imaginable, many that would never have been considered possible for girls before the emergency.

One of my friends, Priscilla Hext (née Holman) contributed this episode in her life as a Wren armourer:

"The year 1942 was rushing to its close. I had recently left school for the last time and, with my parents' support, I applied to join the WRNS. Remarkably quickly I was instructed to go to Plymouth for an interview. My mother and I caught a train from Truro and I had soon signed up for the 'duration'.

"Christmas was at home and shortly afterwards I was back on Truro station, this time catching a train for Mill Hill in North London, a reception centre for Wrens. It was an enormous school with very large rooms which we had to call cabins, and we were on bunk beds. In an interview I applied to join Boats' Crew, but alas that category was full up. They offered several jobs, but none appealed so they gave me an aptitude test – this was quite fun and I enjoyed doing it. Next day I was sent to see a lieutenant commander, Royal Navy, who told me that the test showed I had an engineering aptitude, so would I like to join the Fleet Air Arm as an armourer?

"It seemed the best offer so far, so I said 'Yes'. He told me that I would be dealing with guns and bombs on aircraft on training airfields where young sailors would spend some time before being posted to aircraft carriers. Initially I would go for training in Newcastle-under-Lyme in the Potteries in Staffordshire. So a few days later, I left behind learning how to salute and march and various other navy occupations, and caught a train with 14 other girls all heading for the same course.

"We were met by a navy-blue bus which took us to the Wren HQ, where we were told we were going to live in billets in the town. The other girls had all been in the same cabin in Mill Hill and had paired up, so I agreed to take the single billet. We set off again in the bus with a Wren officer in charge.

"My hostess was out, so the officer left a note and I went with two girls who were just down the road. They were shown up to the bedroom, but there was a horrid smell in the room. We had a good search and found it was the double bed; it was wet and smelly and quite unusable. We thought that the baby we had seen downstairs had probably been put in the bed with insufficient nappies. Betty and Pam decided to try and sleep in the two armchairs and complain next day.

"When my hostess arrived I went back with her to my billet. It was a much smaller house with a kitchen and sitting room downstairs and bathroom with loo upstairs, a tiny room with a cot for the little boy and a bedroom with a double bed. It was obvious that I was to share the bed with Mrs Kay. She told me that her husband was in the army overseas. In spite of these unusual circumstances, I slept very well and Mrs Kay gave me a very nice supper and a good breakfast, too.

"When the bus came I was all ready to go, as were Betty and Pam. They had their luggage with them, very sensibly, as they had had a very uncomfortable night and hardly slept at all. They needed a better billet very badly, so I said I would not complain too much in case billets were limited. When we got to the Wrenery it was chaos, with lots of girls complaining about their billets, and the petty officer who had done the billeting was in tears. I made my complaint, but as I said I did not mind staying where I was for now, I don't think it was ever recorded.

"After lunch, we were taken to where we would be starting our training next morning. We met the three chief petty officers who were to be our teachers, a delightful trio who seemed not a bit put out at the thought of coping with a bunch of girls. They outlined what we would be doing and showed us some Browning guns – and said we would have to strip them and put them together while blindfolded. I think we thought they were joking.

"At the weekend I wrote to my parents, and told them where I was (it wasn't secret), and what I was doing as I had not written since I left home. I told them all about Mrs Kay and how I hoped her husband would stay overseas, with lots of exclamation marks!!!

"That weekend I started a cold, and it was Arctic weather which did not help. In a few days I felt really ill, so Mrs Kay rang the

Wrenery from the kiosk down the road. The navy doctor came and told me to stay in bed; however an ambulance soon turned up and in spite of my arguments carted me off to the Wren sickbay. I was put to bed and the fierce navy nurse called me Priscilla instead of my surname (Holman). She also asked me if I wanted a cup of tea. The occupants of the other beds all peered out from under their blankets, all bleary-eyed from flu and illness, to see what on earth was going on and why I was being so favoured. I hadn't a clue.

"The next thing that happened was that my mother turned up. I think that my greeting was something like 'What are you doing here?' I thought my elder brother in MTBs (Missile Torpedo Boats) must have been killed. However, it turned out that my father was deeply concerned at my billeting arrangements and had been ringing the Commander in Chief, Western Approaches, whose office had put him on to the Chief Wren Officer for Western Approaches. She had spoken to the local Captain Royal Navy who had laid on his car and Wren driver to greet my mother at the station and had booked her a room at the best hotel Newcastle had to offer. I was amazed and really rather horrified at all this and even more concerned when my mother said that my father had given my letter to his friend, Commander Peter Agnew RN, MP for Camborne/Falmouth, who was on the night train for London. I was told that Peter later asked a question in the House: 'Were the Lords of the Admiralty aware that Wrens were being billeted where they had to share their landlady's bed, and did they really think this was suitable?' Unfortunately I do not know their answer.

"The result of all the billeting errors that affected quite a number of girls was that the billeting officer had to face a court martial. She admitted that she had not gone upstairs in any of the houses she was supposed to inspect. I cannot remember what happened to her, but she passed out of our lives.

"Once out of sickbay and now given a bed in the Wrenery, I had a job to catch up on the gunnery lectures. First we dealt with the Browning .303, learning to strip, clean and put it together again, load its magazine and how it would be set up in the wing of an aircraft. Then it was on to ammunition and the proportion of the different sorts – ordinary, tracer, armour piercing etc to be put in the magazine. We all kept very comprehensive notebooks and sadly, years later, I had mine in my tool box, and an oil can leaked all over it and I threw it away.

"We went on to Browning 5s, to Vickers guns, to bombs and detonators, to depth charges and how to set the depth mechanism. It was very comprehensive, but most of us found it fascinating. The three old chiefies were so patient and helpful, so pleased when you got something right and devastated when wrong.

"I enjoyed living in the Wrenery and I made a lot of friends, some of whom I am still in contact with more than 60 years later. We all passed the exams at the end of the course and everyone was very pleased with us as it had been an experiment to train girls; the antis (of which there were quite a few we gathered) had to climb down.

"There were Fleet Air Arm airfields all over the British Isles, and we supposedly were allowed to choose. In fact, I was the only one who went anywhere near their choice. I chose St Merryn in Cornwall, not far from my home. I have often wondered if I had a mark against my name as one to watch, having a father not afraid of taking on admirals or even Lords of the Admiralty!!! We shall never know.

"St Merryn was a lovely place with lots of very nice people and I enjoyed the work. It wasn't so good in the winter when the cold made life a misery. There were few hangars, so the aircraft mostly lived out on dispersal. To deal with the guns, taking them out or returning them, entailed sitting on the wing with the cold biting through the seat of our trousers and every knuckle at risk as we wrestled with the heavy guns. The armoury was kept warm though, and had excellent benches to work at. It was all a different place in the summer and a joy to work outside. The pilots were all very appreciative, even when things went wrong and they had a stoppage. They, like the young men we worked with, were in training before going onto aircraft carriers.

"It was a happy place with frequent dances and entertainments, and the cinema in Bodmin, which we could get to by train from Padstow, was especially popular as there was a café up the street called 'The Chestnuts' which had an amazing supply of eggs for a high tea. I played a lot of hockey and ran for the armoury team, but after two years most of my friends had gone and I decided to move too. By this time I was a Leading Wren with an officer recommendation on my CV, though I was still too young for that. There was a vacancy at a place called Eglinton in Northern Ireland, so I went there. What a journey that was from Padstow to Stranraer in Scotland, by ferry to Larne and then by train again to Eglinton. Luckily I had labelled my luggage, as I fell fast asleep, but some woman in my compartment woke me up in time as she had seen the labels.

"Eglinton was very different to St Merryn. There I had lived in the Hotel Metropole in Padstow, catching a bus up to the airfield every morning, all very comfortable. Here we lived in a sort of large Nissen hut with rather limited facilities for the number of girls. For work, men and women were separated, each having a smallish Nissen hut but adjacent. I was in charge of the Wrens, but a most objectionable petty officer was in charge of the men. He persistently offloaded the worst jobs on us until I rebelled. I kept a very detailed work sheet for both and, armed with this, I went and saw the armoury officer, but I didn't get much help from him, so I went and saw Commander (Flying). He was most interested in my worksheets, and got his writer (i.e. secretary) to type it out and then I signed it. He said he would recommend me to be a petty officer but 'Paddy' – he was Irish – would still be senior to me. A few weeks later Paddy was moved and peace broke out, and we all worked together and no, I never did get my promotion.

"It was a lovely place to work in the summer. There were no hangars and dispersal was very close to Lough Foyle. After work, we would hide our bikes in long grass and nip over the dyke and have a cool refreshing swim – we always carried bathers and a towel in our tool bags. The biggest event while I was there was after VE Day when lots of U-boats came past as we stood on the dyke on their way to Londonderry. It was a very emotional time."

MARY BROWN, MONICA MCCONNELL AND MARY HILTON JONES

When another friend, Wren Mary Brown (née Bridges), volunteered for a category called 'Maintenance' she had no idea what she was letting herself in for.

"After my initial training at Westfield College in London I was posted to HMS *Excellent* in Portsmouth. I had chosen Maintenance as my category, thinking it sounded fun, but not having a clue as to what I would be required to maintain. It was not until I was sitting with nine other Wrens in a shed on Whale Island that I discovered that Whale Island was a famous gunnery school. The gunnery commander came in to introduce us to Chief Petty Officer Coles, and to tell us that we were to be the first 10 Wrens to become QOLCs (Qualified in Ordnance Light Craft). We took copious notes over the next six weeks and learned how to strip, maintain and reassemble all the guns that the MGBs (Motor Gun Boats) and MTBs (Motor Torpedo Boats) carried. These were pistols, rifles, 0.5 inch machine guns, the Lewis gun, Oerlikon gun and the pom-pom 6 PDR (Personal Defence Rifle). It was all quite fascinating and required the great patience of Chief Petty Officer

Coles, a kindly person who knew that we had not done anything remotely like this before. On Whale Island all male classes had to double everywhere on the island, but as a WRNS class we were allowed to march in an orderly fashion.

"On passing out, we were posted in twos to different bases. I went to Great Yarmouth, HMS *Midge*, where for quite a time we were the only QO Wrens working there with about 20 sailors. Our Wren numbers increased as the months went by, each Wren releasing a man to go to sea. It was an exciting life, although hard and greasy work. We were able to go to sea on gunnery trials, and take a turn in firing some of the guns.

"I have many memories of the base at HMS *Midge* and of the little ships that gallantly went out night after night to fight the E-boats, returning sometimes battered, with men injured and their guns covered in seawater, and QOs waiting to remove all guns for cleaning ready for the next nightly foray."

Monica McConnell (née Macmurdo), a WRNS cine gun assessor, was one of the first Wrens to do her job. She told me about the end of her fortnight's training, when there was a Passing-Out Inspection.

"To this day I look to see if the flaps of my pockets are outside, because one of mine wasn't, and one Chief Officer Dixon, who was about 5ft tall, flipped it out as she passed me without the flicker of an eye.

"We were then given our drafting instructions. One of the reasons I had been able to get out of the Civil Nursing Reserve to join the WRNS was because I had the equivalent of A-Level Maths and I had been told radio mechanic was the likely job for me. As it turned out, I was to become a cine gun assessor with the Fleet Air Arm, and so I landed up at RNAS Yeovilton, HMS *Heron*, which was the biggest Air Arm training centre. It is worth recording at this stage that Chief Officer WRNS at Yeovilton was the youngest one in the service. She was Chief Officer Uprichard, and she was slim, beautiful and very efficient. She was engaged to a Captain Hill, and her steward used to recall that he sent her lemons from which she used to strain the juice and use it for her hair.

"The job of a cine gun assessor was to judge the pilot's skill by looking at the film of the target as it appeared in the pilot's ring site and from the position and angle of the target. Then, taking into account various other data, you would tell the budding pilots where they were going wrong and what remedial action they should take.

"The young men used to come and sit with us while we assessed their films; we worked in the dark with a small light and you could see their intense faces as they watched the films; they were so youthful and full of enthusiasm. Looking back, I don't think we thought much about their future, and I doubt whether that came into their reckoning at their particular time. Yet they were mostly destined to go out to the Far East where the casualties were enormous.

"As I had more advanced maths than the other cine gun assessors, I was given the task of initiating them into the theoretical aspect of air gunnery. I was only a Wren, so I lectured them with sleeves rolled up so they would not realise my very junior status. However, it seemed to serve the purpose as they were much in awe of me. On one occasion a young subbie asked one of my colleagues, 'What is the name of that Wren who gives us lectures?' to which she replied, 'We call her Auntie,' (the reason being that I was about three years older than the rest) to which he replied, 'You might – I daren't!' In fact a friend of mine wrote a poem on the subject:

'This way gentlemen, if you please

Sit down, and please don't yawn or sneeze;

The subbies quiver at the knees

Before Auntie.'"

It is almost impossible to believe this next story, but no one could possibly make it up – and, besides, it has the ring of truth. It is from a very different (and not so happy) Wren armourer air mechanic.

Mary Hilton Jones' story begins:

"I volunteered to join the WRNS. I had just left school, having had a strict and sheltered upbringing and my experience of worldly ways was nil. When I told my grandmother what I had done she said, 'I'm so glad darling, every sailor is a perfect gentleman.' These inspiring words were somewhat tempered by the more practical ones from my mother: 'Even if you don't like it you must stick it out as you won't get a ration book if you run away.'

"So I departed for the initial three weeks' training on a camp on the shores of Loch Lomond. This was strict, things were done at the double, floors scrubbed and rescrubbed, with regular checks for head lice and learning to tolerate the unpleasant catering arrangements. At the end of three weeks we were officially signed on, and I became Wren No 76132 and was told I would train as armourer air mechanic in the Fleet Air Arm.

"This involved five-months' training at a remote naval establishment in Staffordshire named HMS *Eagle*. We learned about all the intricacies of various weapons and how to service them, and

I enjoyed the ordered routine; it was like being at school. Having completed the course, we were despatched to our Fleet Air Arm stations. Mine was Donibristle on the shores of the Firth of Forth.

"It was a vast complex, with all the hangars and different departments widely dispersed in case of a bombing attack. The WRNS were housed in an old shooting lodge in the hills behind camp, transported by lorry to and from the camp. Unfortunately, I damaged my thumb on the journey north and was unable to start work for 10 days, which proved to be the first step down a slippery slope of trouble.

"Eventually I got my orders to join Squadron 14 on the parade ground at 8am the following morning, so set off carrying my heavy tool chest, my bell-bottom trousers flapping wetly round my feet. I finally found Squadron 14 and got a very cool reception from RAF Sergeant Robinson, who clearly did not welcome a female in his ranks. The order came to march off and he ungraciously pushed me into a space and off we went, finally arriving at a collection of large packing crates, one of which had 'Uncle Joe's Snack Shack' chalked over the door. We all piled in and I saw by the light of a few candles stuck in bottles that I was the only female in a group of about 20 men, headed by the hostile Sergeant Robinson. I must have seemed like a creature from outer space, with my attempts of polite conversation not made easier by the fact that they spoke unintelligible Glaswegian.

"Quite soon, Sergeant R solved the problem of my presence by sending me on a variety of missions designed to fill my day. Sometimes these were genuine, sometimes classic leg pullers, but always accompanied by the threat that if I didn't fulfil the orders there would be BIG TROUBLE. It was most exhausting. Hours were spent in trailing after red oil for port lights, bottles to keep mag drops in, matchboxes for air screws (slang for propellers), keys for Davy Jones' Locker and many others, culminating one snowy day in an urgent demand for a 'long weight/wait'. I imagined a sort of dock weight and set off, but the weather deteriorated and I decided I would go straight to the main stores rather than take the endless routes ordered by Sergeant R. I knocked on the Commander's door, and he was charming and smiled when I said I'd come for a long weight/wait. After about quarter of an hour nothing happened, so feeling ominously tearful I asked about the weight/wait, and he said, 'You've been sitting here for about quarter of an hour. I think that's enough don't you?' The humiliation of it all…

"I went on leave, feeling rather low, and on my return was summoned by the Chief Wren Officer, a God-like being who became visible only in cases of dire crisis. She handed me a postcard and asked me if I could explain it. My heart sank as I recognised the red ink and bold handwriting of my mother using her standard method of communication when annoyed. She had written, heavily underlined, 'My daughter is no longer in the same condition as when she left home, what are you going to do about it?'

"Then, in the primmer old-fashioned language of that era, the word 'condition' was a sort of code for pregnancy. This didn't occur to me, but it certainly did to Chief Officer Rumbelow Pierce, who pre-judged the situation without consulting me. She said I must 'tell her all the facts', but drew a blank as there were none, so the padre was summoned with an equal lack of success. After a long delay the Chief Officer returned, and said I was to be transferred that afternoon to another destination to 'await developments'.

"There was no time to say goodbye to friends, and I was worried about my tool box down at Uncle Joe's Snack Shack. We had been warned that the cost of any missing tools would be deducted from our weekly pay of seven shillings and sixpence. A messenger was sent to collect them, and either Sergeant Robinson or my Glaswegian mates had unscrewed the bottom of the box because it was completely empty. I was frantic, as I estimated that I would be in the WRNS for about 25 years paying off my debts. I duly departed and was driven to a grim-looking ex-primary school in Dunfermline. It was a holding depot, a polite name for a remand house for Wrens awaiting discharge, mostly dishonourable, and indeed they had landed some odd fish in their net. I didn't realise any of this at first, and in my genteel ignorance thought that the removal of our shoes in a sack at night meant they were going to be cleaned. I think I was there for about a month; self-preservation was the name of the game. But salvation was at hand in the form of a Wren officer from my first training place in Stafford, who came to inspect the holding depot. She had always been very kind and human.

"She walked along the lines of criminals, stopped when she came to me and asked why I was there. I said I didn't know, and she said she would see me afterwards. She sat me down and asked me if I was pregnant. I can remember to this day feeling as if something was exploding in my head, suddenly realising what all this was about. I was absolutely devastated, and the shame of it lasted a long time.

"Within hours I was transferred to the Signals Department at Rosyth as a trainee coder. It was largely manned by Wrens, the work was interesting and I made wonderful lifelong friends and gradually felt focused again. I still think it was miraculous that I was rescued in the nick of time from discharge (you were automatically dismissed when four months pregnant). I cannot bear to imagine my mother's reaction if I had arrived home plus the mythical little stranger and minus the ration book.

"My powerful aunt instigated an enquiry into the affair, and was told that due to a 'clerical' error I had been committed to the tender mercies of Sergeant Robinson. It was essentially a job for a man and my name had got on to the wrong list, so I didn't exist as anyone's responsibility for three months. I suspect that he probably did quite well out of it with a new collection of tools and my daily tot of rum as issued to sailors. It was all such a long time ago but remains astonishingly vivid, and certainly propelled me into adulthood with an enduring curiosity and some realisation of what the outside world was like."

A Wren classifier, another very technical category, now gives an unusual slant on Wren experiences, which I hadn't come across before.

Catherine Avent 2/0 WRNS rtd. wrote to me:

"I joined the WRNS on 29 July 1942 immediately after graduating with a degree in English from Oxford; I have a vivid memory of that first night in the initial training depot at Mill Hill as we were the first batch of recruits. Knowing no one, we were roused by the air raid sirens and taken in the dark down to the basement where we waited for the all-clear signal to be escorted back to our cabins.

Within minutes a quarters officer appeared with a trolley of tea; a simple action which inspired lifelong respect for the way the navy looks after its personnel.

"I had hoped to be a photographer, but there were no vacancies so I found myself at Marconi's labs at Great Baddow, training to be a classifier. (Linguists and special writers became known as classifiers, and after an eight-week course their duties were connected with the observation of the ionosphere and analysis of wireless telegraphy transmissions.) We wore 'bunting tossers' crossed flags', (as category badge), and were considered part of Naval Intelligence. I spent most of the year there working in a little hut three fields away from the building, which meant walking past sleeping cows to get a meal at three in the morning when on middle watch. The house we lived in had a stoker to maintain the boilers. Imagine the excitement when one day a signal came ordering 'Stokes' to report to the Royal Naval Barracks at Chatham to 'stand trial on a charge of bigamy!' We had eyed the aforementioned gentleman suspiciously at mealtimes as he described his wife and kids at Plymouth, and second wife and baby in Malta, from which posting he had been sent home to the UK; only later I realised what a sense of humour the drafting commander had, to post him to an inland Wrenery!

"An unfortunate capacity for mimicry led to my being caught by the second officer in charge, who, not unreasonably, punished me with a whole month's confinement to barracks; halfway through, my posting to the Officers' Training Course came through – so my only distinction in five years' naval service was to be the only cadet to be sent for officer training while being thus punished!"

Christian and John on their wedding day (15th Dec 1943)

MARRIAGE

Somehow, in the course of the autumn of 1943, John and I managed to meet certain members of each other's families and it was decided we could get married when HMS *Oribi* was due for a boiler clean just before Christmas, and John could count on a week's leave. My mother made arrangements for the church, St James's, Spanish Place, in London, where a family friend, Father de Zulueta, would take the service.

One important problem to solve was a wedding dress and a few extra clothes to form a trousseau of sorts. My trousseau was limited by the number of clothes coupons available, because clothes rationing was still very much in force. However my mother cleverly found me an elegant second-hand white velvet garment for a wedding dress, advertised in the Country Gentleman's Association magazine. I was not able to try it on because I was still in Belfast but it more or less fitted and it cost £7. Fortunately, no coupons were required for second-hand items. My mother sold it on again in the same column after the wedding.

Once the church had been booked and my dress acquired, my mother sent out the invitations and we crossed our fingers that the bridegroom would appear. By the greatest good luck, he did.

My father and I drove to the church together. I remember him taking the car around a roundabout several times, to give him the opportunity to say to me that while my wedding was just moments away, I should not be afraid to let him know if I didn't want to get married after all.

"It doesn't matter if you want to change your mind," he said. "It isn't too late and I won't be in the least bit upset."

Needless to say, I had not changed my mind and John and I were married on December 15 1943 as planned, with John looking very handsome in his uniform. I carried a bouquet of white lilies. We held our reception at the English-Speaking Union nearby.

Dried fruit was very hard to come by at the time, but various friends and relations donated enough for the wedding cake which was made by Searcy's, a well-known catering company in Sloane Street, which is still in operation today. An old friend lent us his small green baby Austin for our honeymoon, which we began at The Savoy before driving to a place near Oxford.

After our honeymoon, John returned to join *Oribi* for her boiler clean in Falmouth and my senior Wren officer friend, Nancy Osborne, still in touch, kindly found me a temporary job in the naval plot in the same port at HMS *Forte I* (where we could work in five watches – always a luxury) so that John and I could be together for a little longer. We found a farm house called Little Bosthavick where John and I could stay and where we were indulged in Cornish cream and other local treats.

Baths were taken in front of the kitchen fire and the loo was at the bottom of the garden where curious cows would come to investigate.

The plot at Falmouth, which came under the Commander in Chief Western Approaches, and which I already knew, was very exciting. So much activity was taking place. A great many German E-boats would dash over and do as much damage as possible to shipping either in the Channel or, very cheekily, near our coast and ports. These E-boats were usually picked up by the radar plot and action would be ordered to pursue them. By this time, we were using the magnetron radar which gave a high degree of plotting precision.

Our fate was always in the hands of Their Lordships of the Admiralty.

As John had survived almost everything the Atlantic could throw at him, he was allowed a respite from the violence of the elements and the enemy and appointed to a 'working up centre', suitably named HMS *Mentor*. It was to be found at Stornoway, the principal town of the Isle of Lewis in the Hebrides, about as far as you can get from civilisation; it was not ,however, beset with enemy action – as yet – and therefore might be called peaceful.

His relief, who arrived in Falmouth to take over *Oribi*, wanted to do the handover at sea. *Oribi* was ordered to Scapa Flow, which meant an amazing 2,000-mile non-stop journey for John – from Kirkwall to Inverness by air, then from Inverness to London and on to Falmouth by train. I had some leave, so we travelled back together to London, to Inverness, then to Kyle of Lochalsh and finally by steamer to Stornoway – almost as far as you can go in the UK.

The object of John's activities would be to train reserve and hostilities-only officers (who were to command the large numbers of new escorts now being commissioned) in how to organise, handle and run their ships and work them up, ready for action as convoy escorts.

Stornowegians are a unique race. They were mostly Wee Frees – a minority of the Free Church, which refused to join the United Free Church in 1900. Their religion interfered with their lives and everyone else's. On a Sunday, for instance, any sort of activity was breaking the Sabbath – writing a letter, bicycling, even gardening; such hobbies were deeply disapproved of, and disapproval could result in dismissal from accommodation. One naval officer publicly proclaimed himself a Jew so he could continue with his weekend gardening. John noticed on his walk to matins at the Episcopal Church of Scotland, that all the blinds would still be drawn mid-morning in the houses by the roadside and were still undrawn on his return. They would only be opened in time for evening service at the Free Kirk. John suspected – cynically – that the cause of this was not so much religious enthusiasm but more the result of very hard drinking on the previous Saturday night.

Having decided to try my hand at being a housewife, I found a small flat to rent and set about some cooking. My life so far had not even included boiling an egg, so I had to borrow a cookery book from one of the destroyers which gave a variety of recipes for steak and kidney pudding, plum duff and other naval favourites. Unfortunately, they were all intended to feed 240 men, and it was difficult to work out a suitable portion for a modest two.

After a good deal of division I decided not to try both at once, but to have a go at the steam pudding, having started the meal with kippers – which were the staple diet at all meals in Stornoway and did not require much culinary skill. When I had bought the required ingredients, I mixed them up as instructed and, allowing what I supposed was enough room for it to rise, I wrapped it up in a vest (ex-Wren issue – surplus to requirements), put it in a large saucepan to boil and started to read my book.

What I hadn't grasped from the naval cookery book was how long to allow this much divided pudding on the stove, so I left it on until kipper time, thinking the rather unattractive looking gluey lump would be better for overcooking than under. When the moment came, I was quite unable to tell if it was cooked or not; I had a feeling it was supposed to rise or alter in some way, but it looked much the same as when I had put it in. I gave some to John, who luckily seemed to think it was cooked and ate quite a lot, remarking that it was good and filling.

Another recipe I had rather forced on me by the butcher when he kindly gave me a sheep's head, which was not only without coupons, but free. My heart sank as I read the cookery instructions: 'remove the brains and tongue'. It didn't seem to have eyes – thank God! I persevered. 'Soak it for 12 hours, changing the water repeatedly. Boil it for 4 hours, add some veg and herbs, reboil it for 2 hours – it was still grinning at me and every saucepan in the kitchen was now covered in a sort of green slime; further suggestions: 'the brains can be used for brain cakes' (that's tea taken care of), and 'only a small portion of the head need be served in the broth, the rest can be served separately with the tongue and brain sauce'. This should have lasted us for a week, but just as we were about to taste the first morsel, I began to feel quite hysterical when I suddenly remembered its teeth! Oh, for M&S ready-cooked meals!

John, meantime, was having great trouble with his training courses. The local laird insisted on having only his local country-men as his crew, and communicating with them from the bridge exclusively in Gaelic. By the time he had interpreted to John what he was telling them to do, and John had told him that his orders would result in catastrophe, the crew had got rather bored and started fishing.

Another of the jobs John took on was recruiting officer for the Hebrides, when the proper officer had gone sick. When called up, all the young men of the island opted for the navy and were accepted on principle. Knowing, however, from personal experience that all the superb Hebridean seamen-fishermen had long since been absorbed into the service and were serving in trawlers, these men now being called up were from inland crofts, knew nothing about the sea and were too slow to learn, so he sent them all into the army. An irate major came all the way from Scottish Command to remonstrate with him!

When my leave was over, I returned to Belfast while John remained in Scotland, still eating kippers. It's perhaps unsurprising that John said of the period...

"I thought I would never want to see another kipper in my life."

MOUNTBATTEN AND THE RETURN TO FRANCE

Ever since Mountbatten's personal summons from the Prime Minister to take over command of Combined Operations in October 1941, the total focus was to be the reinvasion of France.

Mountbatten was a brilliant man and his career in the Royal Navy had been meteoric and very much based on his passion for communications. He had specialised in signals, coming top in the higher wireless course at Greenwich. He not only became a radio and radar expert second to none, but was able to persuade the Admiralty to employ Typex machines, which were to transform the navy's entire code and cypher system.

Mountbatten's Combined Operations Headquarters was now at Richmond Terrace, Whitehall, where he developed a new department of Experiments and Operational Requirements. This bulged with the finest brains of the day, and many ingenious ideas were conceived and planned there, as experts of every dimension worked towards a single vast operation – codenamed Overlord – the invasion of Europe.

Among these brilliant boffins beavering away was Professor Solly Zuckermann, the anatomist and authority on apes, known colloquially as 'The Monkey Man', having written a book called *The Sex Life of the Primates* (which became a bestseller among those who supposed it to refer to archbishops!).

Another of the amazing scientific geniuses was Geoffrey Pyke. The problem which faced him was how to provide air protection for seaborne landings beyond the reach of fighter cover based in England, when there was a lack of aircraft carriers. Pyke demonstrated that it was technically possible to construct floating platforms from a mixture of seawater and sawdust frozen together to make a material called Pykrete, which could be used as seaborne airfields. The project was christened Habakkuk.

Mad as this scheme sounds it was very much on the tapis, when Mountbatten sought and got permission to demonstrate to the high and mighty the comparative resistance of an ordinary block of ice with a block of Pykrete. Large samples of each were wheeled into the room and Mountbatten fired at them in turn with his revolver: the ice splintered as you might expect, while the bullet fired at the Pykrete ricocheted round the room. His point was taken and he was not asked for an encore!

However it was here that the concept of an artificial, prefabricated harbour with floating piers was born. Churchill wrote an historic memo to Mountbatten: "They must float up and down with the tide. The anchor problem must be mastered. Let me have the best solution worked out. Don't argue the matter. The difficulties will argue for themselves."

This marked the very beginnings of the immortally famous 'Mulberry'. This was the codename for the floating harbours that would be used for the invasion of Normandy. Their construction had to be hidden from enemy reconnaissance aircraft, and this was achieved by building individually (and temporarily sinking for concealment) each of the 73 concrete and steel caissons, breakwaters, pontoons and floating landing ramps, in different ports throughout the UK, to be raised and towed into place for final assembly off the Normandy coast. The most spectacular of these constructions measured 60 by 17 metres and was the height of a five-storey building. The icing on the cake was PLUTO, the Pipe Line Under the Ocean from the Isle of Wight to Cherbourg. Eventually there were 11 such pipelines across the Channel which kept pace with our Allied armies' advance inland.

None of this was known to any of us Wrens at the time. Although we observed the frequent visits of our Prime Minister, and the mysterious comings and goings of the scientists, it was not until years later that I realised that this building in Whitehall was actually the engine house of Overlord, and all that was to follow. Though we could not see the bigger picture, we could not fail to sense the urgency in the atmosphere, humming with activity. Here, deep in a tiny office in the basement, I was assigned my own part in this huge jigsaw puzzle.

It was on 24 February 1944 that I took up my new position at HMS *Odyssey* in London. My job came under the command of Rear Admiral H. E. Horan, Landing Craft and Bases (RALB). I was to be working on the actual maps of the planned landings and I was so sworn to secrecy that I could not even tell John what I was doing. Many of us were working on individual pieces of the enormous jigsaw; these were necessary preparations, but none of us knew or ever discussed what the others were working on.

The choice of location on the French coast for our assault was a most sensitive subject and an even more deadly secret than most, because the great debate between the planners, which had been going on for months, (and which had equally obsessed our baffled German enemy), was about where we were going to land – was it to be the Pas de Calais area or the Normandy coast, the Baie de Seine? Once the decision was taken to rule out the former, our efforts were concentrated on deceiving the enemy into believing that the Pas de Calais was, in fact, our main objective. The most important element of the deception operation (codenamed Fortitude) was played by the Double-Cross agents, whose object was to persuade Hitler that the Normandy landings would be a feint, and that the real assault was to be mounted on the Pas de Calais by a completely fictitious First US Army Group.

Dummy invasion craft were planted in east-coast ports and mobile wireless vehicles travelled round south-east England broadcasting messages from a number of different locations to fool the German radio interception units. Bletchley Park was much involved in all this.

Even David Niven was involved in an elaborate ruse to throw the Germans off the scent. Niven was a friend of M. E. Clifton James, an Australian actor, who had served in the army in World War One and fought at the Battle of the Somme. At the beginning of the Second World War, he rejoined the army as a second lieutenant in the Royal Army Pay Corps.

Throughout the war, Clifton James continued to act in troop entertainments. Among the roles he took on was a brief cameo as 'Monty'. His striking resemblance to the great man did not go unnoticed and he soon received a message from Lieutenant Colonel Niven of the Army's film unit, asking him to travel to London to make a film.

In fact, Clifton James was to reprise his role as Monty in a plan called Operation Copperhead. For a while, he shadowed Monty's staff to learn more about his mannerisms and way of speaking. To make sure that Clifton James looked as much like the General as possible, he had to wear a prosthetic finger to hide the fact that he'd lost a digit during the First World War.

The plan came to culmination on 25 May 1944, when Clifton James flew to Gibraltar on Churchill's personal aircraft. Once there, he made several public appearances in the guise of Monty, where he talked about the Allies' plan to invade southern France. This was picked up by German Intelligence who quickly scrambled to find out more.

Churchill himself travelled to Dover and walked up and down the famous cliffs in plain sight of German telescopes on several occasions to give the impression that he was looking out to Calais with the intention of landing there. While the Germans were thus distracted, the Allies' actual plan, to land in Normandy, gathered pace.

Meanwhile, in my tiny office beneath the stairs in Whitehall, I was making maps of the genuine landing places for the invasion. The locations were pinpointed for me on large-scale maps of France.

My particular brief was to delineate everything that could be seen on every compass bearing, from each landing position and from the bridge of an approaching landing craft. This was so that any of our men approaching the coastline could use my map readings for identifiable confirmation of where they were – whether that was a main road, a chateau or a station. They would have my maps in front of them for reference.

The big Ordnance Survey maps were spread out on the wall, and showed railways, roads, churches, castles and every possible feature that would be visible to an incoming invader, and from every angle. It was intense and exciting work and obviously detail was vital. It was crucial that the maps were 100% accurate.

There was an atmosphere of tension and excitement in the building as the weeks went on. Occasionally, I would actually see Winston Churchill himself on the stairs on my way into work. I can only imagine what sort of pressure he must have been feeling.

This was the beginning of the crescendo to D-Day and the senior commanders and the main offices of Combined Operations – now to be called Allied Expeditionary Force Advance Headquarters – moved from Whitehall to the even more secret location of Southwick House, a mansion near Portsmouth, from where the invasion landings were directed by General Eisenhower, General Montgomery, Air Chief Marshal Tedder, and the Allied Naval Commander Admiral Ramsay.

My work on the D-Day plans made me long for the historic landing which I knew must be about to take place. The most favourable date had long been chosen, the tide would be right but of course, when it came down to it, the weather – always to be the deciding factor – was bad.

D-DAY

So many different and quite brilliant people were involved in the planning of D-Day, but little is known of the man of whom it might be said saved the whole operation from disaster. That man was Group Captain James Martin Stagg, the Allies' chief meteorological adviser – the weatherman.

It was Group Captain Stagg who had to break the news to the Allied generals, including the formidable US General Dwight D Eisenhower, that there would be a storm on 5 June 1944, the day that had been chosen for the Allies' return to France. June 5 promised a full moon coinciding with low tides, but a successful landing on the Normandy beaches would still depend on clement weather. If the landing craft set out in a storm, such as Group Captain Stagg now forecast, they might be blown off course and low cloud would hamper any air cover. Furthermore, the troops would all be sea-sick by the time they reached the shore and had to be at their best.

Stagg worked with a team comprising meteorological experts from the Royal Navy, the Met Office and the USAAF. This was long before satellite imagery and computer modelling and Stagg's team could only work with direct observations gathered by military and civilian weather watchers. Most of those observations were taken from the land, but some were made from the air by operations such as that run by the RAF's 518 Squadron, which was based on the tiny island of Tiree, in the Western Hebrides. Every day the squadron flew hundreds of miles over the Atlantic in specially equipped Halifax bombers to gather meteorological readings regarding air pressure and temperature that could not be taken from weather stations on the ground.

The missions that 518 Squadron flew, which had to be undertaken in all conditions, were gruelling and dangerous – as many as 10 aircraft and their crews were lost to bad weather in 1944 – but their work was of paramount importance, as D-Day would demonstrate.

When he learned of the storm heading for the Channel on June 5, Group Captain Stagg immediately informed Allied Supreme Command. Unfortunately, the US weather forecasters saw the situation differently and Stagg had quite the battle to convince General Eisenhower to delay the landings by one day.

However, the story does not end with General Eisenhower accepting Group Captain Stagg's advice. If the landings could not take place on June 6, the tides would mean they had to be delayed for a further two weeks. Right along the south coast of England, 5,400 assault craft with 156,000 men were aboard and at sea, all waiting for the magic word 'GO'. Thus, having persuaded everyone that June 5 would be too stormy, Group Captain Stagg continued to refine his prediction.

Without the technology we now take for granted, it was difficult to predict the weather more than two days ahead, but a solitary observation taken 600 miles west of Ireland appeared to show a rise in surface pressure, which could mean a break in the weather. Group Captain Stagg used that single data point to predict the appearance of a high-pressure ridge in the English Channel that would give the Allies just enough time to go ahead in the early hours of June 6. He returned to the Allied commanders with this new information, knowing that if he was wrong, his mistake might cost thousands of lives. It's hard to imagine the weight of that responsibility.

When Group Captain Stagg met the Allied commanders in the early hours of June 5, the storm he'd forecast was already raging and it must have been very hard to believe his new prediction would come to pass. Thankfully, Group Captain Stagg was right.

And so it happened that shortly after midnight on 5 June 1944, Operation Overlord swung into action.

The Allies began the operation with an airborne assault, landing more than 24,000 British, American and Canadian paratroopers behind enemy lines. They also landed a number of bales of straw near Calais, knowing that German radar would register each bale as a paratrooper! The objective was to cause confusion. At 6.30am on the morning of June 6, the amphibious landings began along a 50-mile stretch of the Normandy coast, that had been divided into five sectors: Gold, Juno, Omaha, Sword and Utah.

The Double-Cross agents continued to work hard. One of the most notable of these agents was Juan Pujol Garcia, who went by the codename 'Garbo'. He reported to his German handlers that the Allies were heading for Normandy: too late for the Germans to act on the information. This gave credibility to Garbo's next snippet of 'intelligence' which was that the Normandy landings were merely a feint and that the 'real' attack was still planned for the Pas De Calais. Because Garbo's information on Normandy had been correct, Hitler and the Nazis were convinced that a bigger landing at the Pas De Calais would be next. Thus Hitler ordered two of his divisions there rather than sending reinforcements to Normandy.

Some 7,000 naval vessels were involved in the sea-borne part of Operation Overlord, which was codenamed Neptune. Gold and Sword beaches were the responsibility of the British 50th and 3rd Divisions respectively. Juno was tackled by the Canadian 3rd Division, Utah, the US 4th Infantry Division and Omaha, the US 1st and 29th Infantry Divisions. More than 130,000 troops were landed that morning. Meanwhile, troops from Australia, New Zealand, Belgium, Czechoslovakia, the Netherlands, Norway, Poland, France, Greece and Rhodesia provided invaluable additional support by air, ground and sea.

It was not an easy task to land on those beaches. The weather continued to be a problem, with strong winds blowing landing craft off target. Some of the troops landing at Utah were blown off course (though thankfully to a less heavily defended part of the coast). There were mines in the shallow water and obstacles buried in the sand. German gunners peppered the Allies all the while. The American troops landing at Omaha faced the most experienced and comprehensive German defences and suffered the greatest number of casualties.

While the Germans were taken by surprise on that first day, thanks to Operation Fortitude, and continued to believe that the Pas De Calais would be the site of more landings for quite some time to come, initially the Allies failed to achieve all their objectives.

While progress had been made on all five beaches, Bayeux and Caen remained in German hands. It would take weeks for the Allies to gain a proper foothold in France, via the hard-fought Battle of Normandy that would follow, but D-Day was nevertheless an important turning point. Had that day not been the success that it was, who knows what might have happened. The Allies had one chance to take back northern France and, in doing so, open up the front that would crack Germany's stranglehold on Europe. The importance of Operation Overlord cannot be overstated. The sacrifices made by the young men who lost their lives on D-Day and in the weeks that followed made victory possible at last.

Imagine my thrill when, early on that unforgettable day, 6 June, I heard on my radio that our troops had landed on the beaches that I had so carefully mapped out in that tiny office beneath the stairs. It was a moment I shall remember for the rest of my life.

LEAVING THE WRENS

After a not wholly successful sojourn in Stornoway, John was appointed to his first command, HMS *Broadway*. He was ecstatic with joy and described her as "a typical flush deck, four stacker, a 'cow' in a seaway and with a turning circle like a battleship, but beauty is in the eye of the beholder and she was my very own."

It seemed a convenient moment to announce that I was going to have a baby and also would be able to retire from the WRNS on one of the few grounds over which Their Lordships of the Admiralty had no control.

In the summer of 1944, I found us another flat near Inverkeithing with a superb view of the Forth rail bridge. *Broadway* spent her time patrolling up and down the North Sea, and on every occasion of entering or leaving harbour she had to pass in full view of, and quite close to, our house. Thus, a pre-arranged signal – a bucket hoisted to the crow's nest on a halyard – signified that John would be home for the next meal. What those meals consisted of I have happily no recollection – all I do remember was the terrible day when I inadvertently dropped our fortnightly egg.

Our daughter Felicity Anne was born in the autumn. It was wonderful to be able to spend our first Christmas as a family, but it wasn't long before the Admiralty disturbed us again. On January 1 1945, John was appointed to the command of an Algerine minesweeper, HMS *Moon*, part of the 8th Mine-Sweeping Flotilla in the Mediterranean. Needless to say he would become known as 'The man in the Moon'.

John soon left for Naples on a troop ship, writing of his first glimpse of the city:

"'See Naples and die!' Of what, I thought to myself as, cowering on deck in the wind and driving rain, I tried to locate Vesuvius among the lowering clouds. Once ashore, the sense of disillusionment was compounded at the four-star Hotel Royal, to which I had been directed for temporary accommodation, where I was served Lancashire hot pot, with Manchester tart to follow, by NAAFI staff there, instead of the delicious Italian food I had been looking forward to.

"However, that evening I managed to secure a seat in the old royal box at the opera and, with an audience predominantly comprised of American service men and women, heard a superb performance of *Tosca*. At the interval, the tension of its dramatic plot was relieved when a cloud of inflated contraceptives floated down from the GIs in the upper circle."

The following day, John joined HMS *Moon* in Taranto, where she was berthed with the rest of her flotilla, describing her as:

"...a splendid little ship, compact, workmanlike and sea-kindly... fitted with all the latest sweeping gear; not only the long, serrated steel wires, veered from great winches aft and kept at the right depth and angle by a 'kite' and an 'otter' to cut the moorings of contact mines, but also sophisticated equipment to deal with magnetic and acoustic mines."

In early 1945, though the war at sea was all but over, there were plenty of minefields in the Mediterranean that needed to be swept, and John's flotilla was kept very busy off Malta and the west of Italy. By April, the American First Army was waiting near Genoa for what would be the final land offensive of the war and John's flotilla was sent to Leghorn (Livorno) to clear a channel into the port.

John and his crew received a special Order of the Day from Field Marshal Sir Harold Alexander, Supreme Allied Commander, Mediterranean Theatre, telling them, "Final victory is near. The German forces are now very groggy and only need one mighty punch to knock them out for good... You, who have won every battle you have fought, are going to win this last one."

John picks up the story:

"We had to wait a couple of weeks for this 'mighty punch' and were allowed to give short shore leave. There was a lot of army transport of various nationalities milling around from which lifts could be hitched, so many of us visited the Leaning Tower of Pisa which is about 13 miles north of Leghorn; my own ride there in a Brazilian jeep was one of my more alarming experiences of the war. Another 'tourist attraction' was within walking distance to the south; this was the great mausoleum Mussolini had been building for his family. Built of marble and only half completed, it made an extraordinary glistening sight on a hillside overlooking the sea. Within the unfinished walls a few columns had been erected among which lay numerous vast open and empty sarcophagi looking for all the world like the ruins of some fantastic imperial bath house, an impression which Il Duce certainly never intended to give. Great care had to be taken here and everywhere when exploring as the whole area was still riddled with land mines and booby traps.

"Soon a date was received from First Army for our assault mine-sweeping operation into Genoa and Commander (M/S) called his COs together for a conference. Meanwhile the flotilla was stood down and he had the inspired idea of holding this meeting in Florence. Possibly it was a sign of end-of-war euphoria but the northern city was only 55 miles away and there was ample transport hanging about waiting for the final push. So, we had an altogether satisfactory and agreeable conference which still left time to see the pictures at the Uffizi Palace, stroll across the happily undamaged Ponte Vecchio and go to a concert after dinner before returning to our comfortable billets in the splendid Hotel Excelsior. We felt that war had its compensations.

"Next morning, fortified and informed by this memorable meeting, the six captains returned to Leghorn and got on with the war. In fact, the German Navy chose that night for a final attack; under cover of darkness a number of E-boats charged into the anchorage and loosed off torpedoes which all missed. Having been detected by shore and ship radar they were met by a barrage of fire and a fireworks display from star shells and flares. We, in the middle, were more alarmed by the efforts of our own side, in particular by the projectiles which whizzed close overhead from the 3.7-inch AA batteries on shore firing at minimum elevation. I remember thinking, if friends are like that, what are enemies for?

"Genoa fell a few days later and we duly swept our safe channel into the port without untoward incident. At noon (GMT) on May 2 the German Army's unconditional surrender in Italy – which had been signed secretly on April 29 – became effective. "The previous afternoon Hitler had killed himself at his command post in Berlin. On the day of the surrender we all received another Special Order of the Day from Field Marshal Alexander: 'After nearly two years of hard and continuous fighting... you stand today as victors of the Italian Campaign. You have won a victory which ended in the complete and utter rout of the German armed forces in the Mediterranean. By clearing Italy of the last Nazi aggressor, you have liberated a country of over 40 million people. Today the remnants of a once proud army have laid down their arms to you... No praise is high enough... My gratitude and admiration is unbounded and only equalled by the pride which is mine in being your Commander-in-Chief.'"

John would later tell me that he was particularly glad to have played his part at the end of the Italian campaign, having come face-to-face with the Italians at Sidi Barrani four years earlier. He said, "Some feeling of gratification was permissible that I was in at the beginning and also at the end."

By this time, we all knew that the war in Europe was drawing to a close and indeed on May 8, the Allies accepted Germany's unconditional surrender from the U-boat genius, Reichspräsident Karl Dönitz, who had become leader of the Nazi Party following Hitler's suicide. We were all overjoyed to hear the news. In London, Trafalgar Square and the Mall were thronged as people gathered to see King George VI, the Queen, the Princesses Elizabeth and Margaret and our Prime Minister Winston Churchill appear on the balcony at Buckingham Palace.

Churchill also gave a speech from Downing Street which was broadcast to the nation. In it, he said, "…we may allow ourselves a brief period of rejoicing, but let us not forget for a moment the toils and efforts that lie ahead."

Quite rightly he reminded us that while the war in Europe was over, the conflict continued in the Far East where many Allied troops were still fighting the Japanese.

Directly after the declaration of victory in Europe, John's flotilla was quickly sent to the Far East to support the effort to defeat the Japanese and end the war there, too. HMS *Moon* was to be based in Hong Kong on mine-clearance duty.

However, John's most memorable anecdote from this period involves not a sea battle but a tooth. He had already lost a front tooth thanks to an accident while on a Russian convoy, when he collided with his ship's compass binnacle during rough weather. Now a tooth further back was aching. When HMS *Moon* stopped at Port Said en route to Bombay, John decided to get it fixed. A local dentist had a dig around but as soon as the flotilla was in the Suez Canal, John's terrible toothache returned.

A consultation with the flotilla's MO, who was on another ship, HMS *Seabear*, ended with the young doctor suggesting John try to fashion a temporary filling with the help of HMS *Moon*'s sick berth attendant. The MO would provide instructions over the radio.

John described the drama that ensued.

"The sick berth attendant (SBA) and I duly took up 'Action Station' in front of a mirror in my cabin under the bridge. He had our limited dental armoury, while my good steward manned the voice-pipe to relay the instructions received by the signalman up top: my steward Stone had also taken the precaution of getting out the brandy!

"Communication was quickly established but the cumbersome R/T procedure made it a very protracted dental operation. Omitting the call-signs of 'Yardley' for *Moon* and 'Arden' for *Seabear*, the exchange of signals began something like this:

From MO: 'Report position of tooth for plotting on dental chart.'

Reply: 'Unable to locate. Whole side aches.'

From MO: 'Tap teeth in turn and see which hurts most.'

Reply: Unprintable but relayed as 'the captain would prefer a less painful method.'

"And so it progressed after a fashion, and we eventually decided that the offending molar was the upper tenth to starboard; but by then the doctor seemed to have given up, although his interest revived when my assistants were able to report triumphantly the discovery of a hole in one tooth in the suspect region. Then, by dint of facial contortions on my part and bodily ones by the SBA, who succeeded in inserting at least part of the vile concoction he had prepared from a recipe in the *Small Ships Medical Manual*. I ordered the signal 'Evolution completed' to be sent to the MO, but did not feel much better.

"A signal was then sent to NOIC Aden, our next stop 1,300 miles away, giving our ETA and requesting an urgent dental appointment for the CO on arrival. There would be scant time for this as the two ships were scheduled to stay there only long enough to fuel, but everything went splendidly; a car was waiting at the landing place and in no time I was sitting thankfully in the dental chair. With a cheerful, 'We'll soon put that right for you, old man,' the naval tooth-wright jabbed the needle in for an injection and within 10 minutes I was on my way again minus a tooth.

"An hour later, steaming eastwards, the anaesthetic wore off and it was only too painfully obvious that the wrong tooth had been extracted. Next stop Bombay, 1,650 miles!"

PACK AND FOLLOW

With John at sea, I occupied myself staying first with my mother, then my mother-in-law. My mother lived in a thatched cottage in Suffolk and although she liked the idea of having us to live with her and getting to know her first grandchild, the reality didn't quite match up and interfered with her rather well-planned life.

Luckily, my mother-in-law, Lottie, who lived in Woking, adored having us and spoiled Felicity horribly. But there came a moment when we all needed a change and just for fun, and in desperation, I took a job (advertised in *The Times* agony column) as companion help to a lady in the Lake District near Ambleside.

The lady in question was going to pay me plus my keep, but having a shrewd suspicion that I wasn't going to be much help, though I could be a companion, I declined the pay. How right I was. Looking after Felicity, it seemed to me, was a full-time job. Also, I had no idea how to clean a house (and it was a big house) or even my room properly, so Mrs Barbara Bankhurst taught me everything I know about housework which has been extremely valuable all my life. We got on fine once I became slightly more useful and she loved Felicity, who thrived in the lovely lakeside air.

After a few months, Mrs Bankhurst decided to go away for a visit and told me to invite a friend to stay. I found a school friend called Anne Lee who jumped at the idea. I was a bit nervous about the responsibility of the house, and Anne had even less idea of housework than me.

All went well until the last day when Barbara was expected back and the Aga went out. I found the instructions, I followed them minutely but nothing seemed to work – then I had a brilliant idea. I reversed the Hoover so that instead of sucking, it blew and I held it into the Aga's entrails, making a very violent draught until the whole thing was practically red hot. Somehow it did not blow up or set fire to the house so when Barbara returned, there was her beautiful Aga looking quite normal – but perhaps a bit hotter than usual.

Soon after that, I left and went back to my mother-in-law; and while staying with her I decided to buy a car.

During the war, people received money instead of wedding presents as there was very little alternative choice at that difficult time; by then in my Post Office Savings Account was quite a little nest egg. After some research I found a beautiful small blue car which seemed to be just what I wanted. It was a Ford 8 and belonged to a doctor at the local psychiatric hospital who wanted £250.

I rang my father, now retired, to ask what he thought.

"Don't touch it," he said. "You could have bought it for £50 before the war."

So, of course, I bought it and the doctor kindly delivered it to me.

There was another problem because apart from having a few driving lessons from my grandmother's chauffeur right at the beginning of the war and a couple of attempts in Ruth's car, I had only ever ridden a bicycle. My mother-in-law was therefore vital to my plan as she would have to come with me while I learnt the rules of the road. It would also be her job to keep an eye on Felicity during our travels until I could take my test.

I was very excited by this whole project and well remember the nasty moment when we set out for the first drive. Somehow, we secured Felicity in the back with a few toys (no safety seats in those days); the car only had two doors so it was not unlike a moving playpen, and she wore her little harness. As I bravely put the lever into gear, the whole thing came away in my hand.

Shock horror! I thought, perhaps, my father had been right.

Between us, Lottie and I pushed the lever back into the first gear it would engage; luckily it was a low forward gear and we crept along at about one mile an hour to the nearby garage. Imagine my relief when the mechanic calmed my fears by saying the lever had just become detached and screwed it back securely. That was the only time in the car's life that it had a problem. So, all went well and we sailed about Surrey in great style, exploring the beauties of the county and visiting all our friends.

During the war I had grown up considerably as I plunged headfirst into one unknown job after another. Now I had taken on, with complete but quite unjustified confidence, the lifelong commitment of being a sailor's wife and a mother. But for us ex-Wrens, who had discovered independence and freedom, the world was now our oyster, so when a telegram from John told me to get out to Gibraltar as his whole flotilla of minesweepers would be arriving there in a few weeks' time, I was thrilled.

You might think when you marry your sailor that this legendary gamble (i.e. a wife in every port) is something you could take in your stride; what you may not have taken on board is that there is an even more powerful contender for your beloved's affections than you can ever hope to vanquish – that is his ship. If by any mischance he is the captain, do not delude yourself that you can ever be first for his favours. His ecstatic affection for every nut and bolt of this vessel will be his first thought in the morning and his last at night. Having hoisted in this painful fact early in your relationship, you can resign yourself to being always in second place at best and make the most of what remains.

The phrase 'Pack and Follow' was I think invented by Joy Packer, who published her book of that name in 1945. Although her experiences of pursuing her Royal Navy husband round the world were very different to mine, we certainly would have had a great many similar stories to tell. Noël Coward took up the theme when acting as captain of HMS *Torrin* in the famous World War Two film *In Which we Serve*. His character dines on board just after the ship is commissioned and congratulates one of his young officers who has just become engaged. At the ensuing party, he persuades his wife (Celia Johnson) to give an after-dinner speech in which she reveals to the fiancée some of the trials she will probably encounter in her future life as wife of a dedicated naval officer. Most graphically she alludes to the ever-present competition – her 'Grey Rival', as she puts it.

Having received John's invitation to meet him in Gibraltar, I cleared my bank account and found a Dakota – that ubiquitous, amazing, maid-of-all-work, immortal aeroplane – that would take us, stopping at Lisbon on the way. Felicity, (nearly one by now) travelled in a carrycot for free with most of her possessions under the mattress. She was the only child on board and kept the long-suffering stewardess busy throwing everything out of the cot. It was the first of many journeys we were to make, always frightfully exciting.

Finding myself unmet in Gibraltar as is the norm, (though I did not realise this was to be the norm at the time) I took us off to The Rock Hotel, without enquiring the price. There we lived on bananas and ginger biscuits, which had not been seen in England since before the war, until rescued by the first of the flotilla of Algerine minesweepers, sailing home from Hong Kong to be refitted at this port.

There were four in the flotilla: HMS *Mary Rose, Seabear, Rowena* and *Moon*. Derek Edleston, captain of the *Mary Rose*, was the first to arrive. He made some discreet enquiries on my behalf and, having decided I could not afford any meals in the hotel, kindly invited us down to the dockyard where HMS *Mary Rose* would provide our daily requirements. So, until John arrived, Felicity Anne in her pushchair and I would daily stroll down the steep hill through the town and dockyard and arrive to be looked after most sumptuously in the captain's cabin. Nobody had told me that there was two hours' time discrepancy between England and Gibraltar, so the hotel had found us keeping very strange hours.

It took me some time to realise that naval wives were not actually allowed to live in Gibraltar, the local Gibraltarians being very short of accommodation for themselves. However, there was no chance of us living at The Rock Hotel for much longer so, leaving Felicity Anne in the care of Derek, who found relays of sailor volunteers to babysit, I set off on a doubtful house-hunt.

Gibraltar is a fascinating place. It has been a bastion of the Royal Navy since it was captured by British forces under the command of Admiral Sir George Rooke in 1704. Since then it has been developed as a principal naval base with repair yard and dry docks and is used as a port of call and fuelling port by many commercial steamship lines. In 1492 Catholic Spain had expelled the Jews from its shores, but under British rule the Jewish community was permitted to resettle in this strategically vital southern tip of the Iberian Peninsular for the first time in 200 years. By the mid-eighteenth century, about a third of the population was Jewish, adding to the richly cosmopolitan mix of the free port. Christians, Muslims, Jews and Hindus from England, Spain, Portugal, Italy, North Africa and India live side by side in Gibraltar.

My first small historic find there was a relic of the Battle of Trafalgar. At the end of that historic day, Nelson's body was transported in HMS *Victory* to Gibraltar and placed in a butt of brandy to preserve it for his famous homecoming and funeral in London. But some of our sailors who had died in the same battle had been buried in a seemingly forgotten little cemetery I found, as I explored the route from The Rock Hotel down the steep hill to the dockyard.

The Rock of Gibraltar towered over the whole fortress and above The Rock there was usually a very large threatening black cloud – the *levanter* – so if it wasn't actually raining it looked as if it soon would. If one climbed to the top there were the rather disagreeable monkeys – around 230 Barbary apes – who would daringly snatch anything which one might have left carelessly available. We kept our distance.

Not far from The Rock Hotel I found a wonderful old building which housed a very splendid library, which belonged to the military. Up the front of it climbed the biggest wisteria I have ever seen, with twining trunks fatter than a man's arm. A café had been set up in the garden where children could play safely nearby. I met Nicky Fletcher there, an army captain's wife, who had a little boy the same sort of age as Felicity. Richard was just about walking and I was very jealous as Felicity was still at the crawling stage.

Nicky became a great friend and was a mine of information. Her husband, Sandy, was on the staff of the Governor. Being an army wife, she of course was provided with quarters to live in and had been transported by sea from England in a troop carrier. I thought Felicity would be impressed by Richard and would emulate his walking ability. Imagine my dismay when, instead, Richard decided to go back to crawling. Nicky wasn't frightfully pleased either.

There did not seem to be any rational way to find anywhere to live when one was not supposed to be there, but somehow I came upon a very small flat, its rent just within our means, immediately opposite the police station. It was not strategically ideal but nobody appeared to notice; plus it was the only possible place that was available. It had a very small bedroom entirely filled up with a bed, a small bathroom and a kitchen which was the only place where one could sit. There was a minute gas cooker and that was about all. I moved in and luckily, at that moment, John arrived in his minesweeper HMS *Moon*.

I won't forget that first night. We were awoken by some extraordinary noises – a sort of banshee caterwauling. At first I thought the apes must have moved in too, then other quite unidentifiable noises followed. With the above history of Gibraltar perhaps I should not have been surprised to find that we shared a wall with the synagogue, and that their side of this extremely old building must have been for wailing.

I had also by this time located a nice Gibraltarian lady, Consuelo, who was going to be Felicity's part-time nanny, so I could occasionally go off and take part in Gibraltar's social life, such as it was. Felicity was not best pleased at having both a father and a nanny and I remember her initial disapproval as she crossly disappeared in her pushchair with Consuelo for an afternoon walk.

One problem that had been exercising me was the lack of fresh milk in Gibraltar, largely because there were no cows. So it was a great relief when through Nicky's intercedence, I learned that I was to be given a ration of one gin bottle of milk every other day from the Governor's residence – The Convent – where a privately owned cow was kept.

I was still very inexperienced at housekeeping and having to use the cookery book, borrowed from HMS *Moon*, which gave instructions for naval cooks feeding 200 or so men. It was not as helpful as Nigella Lawson or Rick Stein's delightfully illustrated publications would have been. The minute gas cooker in the flat had practically no pressure during the day so if I wanted to roast anything I had to put it in the oven at bedtime and set the alarm to take it out at about two in the morning – then give it time to heat up for the actual meal.

Derek's wife Norah had arrived by now, closely followed by HMS *Seabear* and *Rowena*, along with Bob Harvey and K.P. – his name was Kirkpatrick but he answered to K.P. Bob's wife was unable to join us all and K.P. was a bachelor. Not having children to contend with, they stayed in hotels and were not faced with such problems as I had, but together we explored all the possibilities of nightlife in the town and found strange sorts of nightclubs and restaurants.

There were endless shortages, and although Spain was just over the border, we were not allowed to shop there. Luckily the Royal Navy was fairly well supplied and we could sometimes dip into their hard rations. Everywhere was still staggering to its feet after the war, which had affected everyone for at least five years, even those not actually fighting.

MALTA

In August 1946, at the end of a big job clearing an extensive minefield in the approaches to Tunis and Bizerta, John left HMS *Moon* and was appointed fleet mine-sweeping officer on the staff of the Commander-in-Chief Mediterranean. John's new boss was Admiral Sir Algernon (Algy) Willis, whose wife was sister to the Rt Hon Clement Attlee, the then Prime Minister.

The promotion meant a move to Malta. Norah and I and Felicity followed John as soon as we could find a ship to take us. John had booked us into the Crown Hotel in Sliema which overlooked the sea. The weather was mostly good on the island though the winter months could feel quite cold, especially as the houses and flats had stone floors and not much facility for heating. We often had meals on the roof which was a novelty. Everything was amazingly cheap and we soon escaped from the hotel into another modest flat.

Living was expensive and accommodation hard to find and the Crown Hotel was anything but luxurious. The whole island had been in naval hands for so many years that the staff had all learnt their skills in the navy; as a result the food served was all from the same old cookery book: bacon and eggs for breakfast, steak and kidney or greasy sausages for lunch and endless figgy duff (suet puddings) with custard for pudding.

There were several other naval families stuck temporarily in this hotel and a row of prams (the babies secured with little harnesses), tightly packed together, graced the front of the building during babies' rest times, while their mothers gossiped in the lounge within earshot. Sometimes when the children woke up, the more active and enterprising of them tried to amuse themselves by throwing their toys at each other or endeavouring to squeeze themselves out of the straps – the others just lay idly, gazing at the sky.

On one memorable occasion I heard loud yells coming from the pram park and rushed outside to investigate. Felicity's neighbouring baby, one of the stationary variety and about the same size as herself, had rather tempting flaccid pale flesh, and Felicity had leaned over and experimentally tried to bite into one of these fat little arms. It clearly had not been as enjoyable as she had hoped, but this would not placate the baby's mother and I was at a loss as to how to apologise.

It was not long after this that Felicity became ill (no connection with the previous episode I don't think). The hotel food was not at all suitable for a year-old baby and it was a real problem what to give her. Her illness became serious and she was taken to the Maltese hospital with dysentery. John was, of course, away, and I had a terrible few days when the doctor told me cheerfully that they were giving her the strongest medicine available which they hoped would kill the bug without killing her as well.

On these sorts of occasion one just sits in the hospital, watching and waiting, willing her to get better. After a few days they told me she was okay. I thankfully took her back to the hotel and for almost a week she would only eat water biscuits. I redoubled my efforts to find us a flat and Felicity was soon eating the sort of freshly cooked food I wanted her to have, and as many water biscuits as she could fit in.

Soon afterwards we found a flat. It was quite near the hotel as it happened and consisted of lovely big airy rooms with huge windows with shutters, stone tile floors and a most attractive flat roof to use for picnics and play – it was a great advance in our lives.

A local girl named Connie became our daily help and nanny, though we often employed sailors as babysitters. We had to be careful doing this, as Connie's fiancé was very jealous. On one occasion, he heard that John's sailor-servant had been in the house on baby-sitting duties when Connie got home. The fiancé insisted on a signed affidavit that nothing untoward had occurred!

Getting about Malta was a problem until John managed to fix a passage for the Ford 8 which travelled for free from Portsmouth to the island in an aircraft carrier. Until this luxurious moment we were dependent on buses which would never depart the stop until they were full. John was constantly occupied paying a penny or so to boys hanging around near the stop to fill it up, so it could start on its way.

Now was the moment when the navy came into its own. We had a very large fleet in those days and it was only necessary for John to send a few signals, discover when the next aircraft carrier was sailing from Portsmouth to Malta and ask if the captain would be agreeable to transport our car to us in Malta. This method was slightly risky because, owing to the indigencies of the service, a ship destined for Malta might be diverted to South America or Hong Kong, but on this occasion she arrived at her scheduled port.

My poor mother-in-law, Lottie, had had to be instructed to drive the car to Portsmouth and deliver it to the said aircraft carrier. This she took in her stride being, like the White Knight in *Alice Through the Looking Glass*, "used to doing at least six impossible things before breakfast".

It was a delight to go to the Grand Harbour at Valletta and find our little car sitting rather forlornly on the dockside; it appeared in good shape apart from its roof, where it must have received some sort of bash which detached a slice – from then on we always had to have a stone on top to keep it from flapping. This however made it very easy to identify if we ever mislaid it.

There were no rules in Malta in those days about taking driving tests or knowing the rules of the road, so I was able to use the car and get quite a lot of experience during the two or three years we were there. There was very little traffic in any case and the only rule agreed by all was that he who hooted longest and loudest won.

Malta was provided with roads of a sort to all the places you might need to go, but the country roads were more suited to donkeys, ponies, goats and carts etc, so you had to drive very slowly, which is just as well, as on taking a sharp corner one day my door flew open and Felicity, standing behind me and holding on to the back of my seat, fell out onto the road. I rushed back to pick her up expecting to find blood everywhere, only to discover she was quite unhurt, frightened certainly, but because I was going so slowly and she fell so loosely and unexpectedly, she had hardly been damaged.

Being a parent for the first time one has a lot to learn and I always felt sorriest for the firstborn as they take the brunt of one's learning experience, being always practised upon!

A bonus to John's job was his associated appointment as Secretary and British member of the Mediterranean International Mine-Clearance Board, which comprised mine-sweeping experts from Allied and ex-enemy navies, who were working together to clear the many thousands of mines that had been laid between 1939 and 1945. This required him to attend quarterly meetings in Rome.

John wrote in his memoir:

"We have enjoyed an harmonious ecumenical existence, my wife and I, since long before that word became popular: in fact, even if we had heard of it when we got married in 1943 we certainly could not have spelt it, and I like to think that over the years we have learned a lot about our beliefs – and particularly where they run in parallel – from each other. So when I, the Anglican half, found myself visiting Rome every other month as Secretary of the International Mine-Clearance Board soon after the war, I felt I was being offered an unfair advantage over my wife who had never been to this, her spiritual home. For her sake and mine, therefore, I set myself three objectives; first, to attend a ceremony in St Peter's; second, to see the new excavations under St Peter's, not yet open to visitors; and third, to obtain an audience of the Pope."

He achieved all three of those objectives. The Holy Father at this time was Pope Pius XII, who kindly agree to grant a private audience to the International Mine-Clearance Board members at Castel Gandolfo.

John wrote:

"It was an unforgettable experience, this reception in the quiet of the Pope's study, where he sat at his desk with us grouped in chairs set close around him. He talked to each of us in our own language, speaking as a man who really knew the world and who cared very much about us as individuals and our countries; the French expression 'sympathique' seems to me to describe his personality better than any English word can. And particularly striking to me in those pre-ecumenical days, was that his interest transcended denominations so that I could not imagine him calling me a heretic, as my wife occasionally did.

"Pius XII may not have been such an extrovert as John XXIII nor so widely travelled and respected world-wide as the present Pope, but I took home with me to my family the indelible impression of having met a unique person of high intellect, totally imbued with holiness and charity, yet who found time to be a little interested in my proxy pilgrimage."

While we were in Malta, my sister Anne and Johnnie came to visit us. They had met in Italy, where Anne was working with the Malcolm Clubs, and had recently got engaged.

Johnnie had been a Blenheim and Mosquito pilot in the RAF, who flew in at least 59 operational sorties, being shot down while serving in the Middle East. He then went on to serve as a marker pilot with 105, the Path Finder Squadron. He was awarded the DFC Royal Air Force, and to quote from the *London Gazette* 22 May 1945 "the courage and tenacity of purpose that he has displayed has been very evident against heavily defended targets in Germany itself."

At this time, Anne planned on her return to England to try to get a job with the BBC. She was quickly absorbed into this organisation and appointed to the Third Programme which was then being established. Later I went to visit her in her office, somewhere off Oxford Street, I seem to remember, and while she was reading the news I made faces at her to see if I could make her laugh!

My memory has left considerable gaps in my long life but I do recall our leaving Malta for home in April 1948, with a new baby, Simon, by now a few months old.

John had been appointed to command HMS *Roebuck*, a destroyer based in Plymouth, so we did a straight swap with the naval couple who took over our flat in Malta, with us moving into their former abode near Bath. *Roebuck*'s duties included acting as an emergency destroyer for the Western Approaches and taking Dartmouth cadets on training cruises. Notably, *Roebuck* provided a high-speed cross-Channel escort for the President of France on an official visit, and also accompanied Princess Elizabeth and Prince Philip to the Channel.

This period in Devon was followed by a span in Pembrokeshire – 'Little England beyond Wales' as it was known. Here we rented an interesting house that only had gas – no electricity. The village was called Dale, right by the sea; the primroses were twice the usual size and there were as many purple-coloured as there were yellow. John was 'showing the flag' to South Wales and occasionally we had to attend functions in Swansea and Cardiff. The first time I had to take John's evening-dress clothes, I forgot the trousers! Not a popular mistake.

SINGAPORE

In 1950, John left destroyers for a new world of diplomacy when he was appointed aide-de-Camp to Malcolm MacDonald, Commissioner-General for South East Asia. This meant a move for us all to Singapore. John went on ahead in one of the very old troop ships.

I sold the faithful Ford, which helped to buy our next vehicle, and prepared to take the family east. John wrote me descriptions of how he organised the naval families in his trooper so that they could sleep on deck (owing to the extreme heat), making their lives more comfortable and getting the sailors to transport the bedding and generally help out. And so, a few months after producing our second son, Martin, I followed.

We were given our passage to Singapore in one of the new army transports, which had been converted from German 'Strength through Joy' vacation ships introduced by Hitler, and taken over by us after the war. The Royal Navy had recently decided to pay the fares of families following the fleet, which was a great boon. There were mostly army families aboard the trooper, who knew their way about. We could have done with John to solve our problems.

It was quite an expedition, with Felicity now five, Simon three and Martin a few months old. To begin with we were given one small cabin with a double bunk. I had the top one and Felicity and Simon were supposed to sleep heads and tails, with a cot attached to their bunk for Martin. I protested that this was a recipe for murder but we had to go on hunger strike before anyone took any notice of us. However, a very nice senior RAF officer (who became a lifelong friend) took up our plight and before long two doctors, who were sharing a three-berth cabin, were ordered to change cabins with us. The doctors had their revenge later, however, when my children, who insisted on eating porridge for breakfast in the Red Sea, which with a following wind was extremely hot, came out in spots and needed to be painted purple by the doctors' cure-all.

After this, things went well, in spite of having to find 11 meals a day (five for the baby, and three each for the children and myself all at different times). We sailed through the Mediterranean, the Suez Canal, the Great Bitter Lake and the Red Sea, then we called at Colombo. We broke down in the Great Bitter Lake and were allowed to swim – it was like floating in hot milk! I might here note that while swimming in this soupy water, my children were looked after by a good-natured nanny – one of the few not being seasick. It was notable that all the senior officers who were travelling with their children and a nanny, were no better off than me; in fact worse as they had to look after their poorly nanny as well as their children!

I was determined to show the children camels, while we were in their country, so we walked miles hunting for tourist places where they offered rides. This was a great success and I took some photographs.

Imagine my surprise when, going through the Suez Canal, we could see hundreds of camels with their children and babies.

At Colombo we were invited ashore by tea planter friends, which was interesting and restful, and where we saw acres and acres of tea plants (which happen to be a species of camellia, *C. sinensis*, my favourite plant) growing on the surrounding hills. It was at this point that the doctors' revenge became apparent when I had to take three purple children to visit our tea planter friends!

John was waiting at the dock side when we arrived at Singapore, with a baby amah (Chinese nanny) and a new car beside him. We went first to a sort of hotel in Singapore town where monkeys visited us in our bedrooms! There was a waiting list for accommodation in the naval base where John would be working in the north of the island, near the causeway to the Malayan mainland.

By good luck we discovered that there was a house available at the Changi end of the island, where the RAF was based; nobody wanted it because it was so far from the naval base, so we pounced and found the most delightful small building in a naval establishment not far from the infamous Changi gaol. Our new car lived underneath the house and the accommodation consisted of two bedrooms and a sitting room which all had rattan blinds which one could wind up and down instead of outside walls, and was kept delightfully cool by old-fashioned ceiling fans rather than the modern air conditioning which I always found too cold.

Thinking back to that house, John wrote of a particularly alarming incident involving our new neighbours:

"Next to us were a cluster of basha huts which housed the staff of the boom defence depot, whose communal privy was in view of our front veranda. One night when sitting out there before bed we heard a great commotion in the latrine, saw its door burst open from which erupted a figure holding up his trousers. Next day all the talk in the kampong was of the tough stoker petty officer who had fled from one of the small, dark cubicles there when he found a large, slimy, scaly creature sniffing his bare legs. Escaping hurriedly, he was pursued by his equally surprised companion: a monitor lizard, the large, harmless, dragon-like reptile that is quite common in those parts."

Our children slept in one room, with the amah lying on the floor at the end of the baby's cot, with her own chosen hard pillow. If Martin so much as turned over she would change his nappy and settle him down again.

Downstairs at the back of the house was accommodation for our staff. I had found Sui and Nan (cook and housekeeper) who were with us for the two and a half years we were there and who moved with us to the naval base, when after two years, a house became available, and we were forced to move. They had two children, and in no time, whatever we had planned, the children all played together; their little girl was about the same age as Felicity but much smaller and always ended up being the fall guy in their games. I never quite mastered what language the children spoke but they seemed to understand each other.

We managed communications with Sui, who was a very good cook. Nan never learnt a word of English but sign language worked wonders. She washed and starched John's white uniform every day; she was also remarkably good at sewing and when John stained one of the lapels of his white dinner jacket and tried to clean it with bleach(!) she replaced it – imagine making a new lapel – just like that!

Another time, when we were preparing to return home to England, I bought about a mile of striped material and, spreading it out flat on the balcony, set about cutting out six pairs of pyjamas. Somehow I managed to produce too many right legs! Nan, smiling in all directions, scooped the whole lot up and next day produced the six finished pairs.

Choosing one's staff had been quite a performance and the choice was considerable; one went to the Labour Exchange in Singapore and there were hundreds of Chinese people of every skill. They all produced much-handled references and it was pot luck picking the most suitable. We already had the baby amah chosen by John; it was likely, therefore, that Sui and Nan would never really get on with her and they always delighted in upsetting her. When she finally left, annoyed just once too often, Sui told me I should have offered her 10 dollars more in her wages, but I think he was feeling pleased with himself for having got rid of her.

We had a rather jolly social life in Singapore. The Governor General, Sir Malcolm MacDonald, lived in a splendid house called Bukit Serene over the causeway on the mainland and had interesting parties which we had to attend. Guests might include royalty, artists, scholars, athletes and civil servants. At a time when it was still very unusual, Malcolm MacDonald set an example by refusing to visit clubs that were not multi-racial, and by entertaining all races equally.

The Governor had a wonderful collection of ancient Chinese jade, which was a pleasure to admire. While he was away, we were allowed the use of his swimming pool which was floodlit from below as he liked a clear view of his girlfriends. His wife lived in Canada so he had a certain amount of freedom to behave as he chose.

The very hot climate suited us and our social life was based very much on the officers club in Changi, where the RAF had their headquarters – there was a *pagir* or protected beach (from sharks), with lovely sea bathing. The sailing club had what was called 'Mem's Day' on Wednesdays which encouraged wives to indulge; I can't describe the pleasure of sailing in such a climate, but it was heavenly and the only other place with comparable boating that we lived in was Malta.

Changi was quite a distance from the naval base and dockyard where John's office was situated; for the last few months of the appointment and during the riots, John went to work by boat which he enjoyed and was more convenient.

There was political trouble while we were in Singapore and riots took place quite frequently in the main town where I went for shopping. One time I was there in the town, driving through the milling crowds which I took to be the result of election upheavals. I didn't realise at the time how dangerous the situation really was. I (and my family) were relieved when I turned up unscathed at home. In spite of this problem, we decided to have a holiday up-country at Fraser's Hill which meant another long drive and a night on the way spent near Kuala Lumpur, where we stayed in a sort of guest house. In the bathroom was an enormous basin and jug full of water. I just dipped the children in the jug as there did not seem any alternative. I never did discover what one was supposed to do but apparently a more sophisticated form of washing was available there.

From there we had to have an armed escort up-country, and for the few miles that this was not provided, we had to carry a loaded pistol. I was not keen to do this, so I drove while John took the revolver. We had hardly started when from the side of the road a monkey leapt out in front which gave us a good fright. We were happy to arrive and spend a week there in the cooler temperatures which did us all good.

Travelling in the mainland part of Malaya reminded one of the war and the disastrous loss of this exact part of the country, when the Japanese had marched unobserved down the long peninsular for several weeks before taking Singapore so easily. For some reason those in command expected to be attacked from the south, and all their defences were directed towards the sea. At this time John was actually escorting a convoy of Australian troops from Colombo, where on the waterfront a great sign proclaimed 'CEYLON TEA IS GOOD FOR YOU'.

As John recounted:

"As the Japanese Army pushed relentlessly down the Malayan peninsular, they got daily nearer Johore – then they were attacking the Causeway and still our men seemed unaware. Then luckily sense finally prevailed and we were ordered to return to Colombo. Later we heard on the BBC News of the final assault by the Japanese on Singapore island. The thousands of Australian troops, embarked in that very convoy that I was helping to escort, must have been surprised as well as relieved to wake up after 10 days at sea and find themselves looking at that same tea advertisement."

When, years later, I went to the museum to look up *The Straits Times* (the local paper) of that period, it was painfully obvious that the headlines concerned local affairs and scandals that were clearly of much more interest than the small paragraph recounting the progress of the Japanese Army approaching from the north, through the Malayan jungle.

TRAVELLING HOME

There was an epidemic of measles at Felicity's school, which Simon unfortunately caught and he became very ill with some complication. He was taken to the local hospital at Changi where he was unlucky enough to catch poliomyelitis or infantile paralysis as it was also known.

Nobody knew much about this deadly illness and the paralysis attacked the back of his neck and shoulder area, leaving him with a partly paralysed ridge and threatening to cause his spine to curve. John's appointment in Singapore was coming to an end, so luckily we were soon on our way back to England where more expert medical advice could be sought.

We decided to break the long sea journey back to England by taking a house up in the hills of Ceylon – now the Republic of Sri Lanka – for a month between troopships, the second of which would get us back to England in time for the New Year, a better time for consulting the medical profession than just before Christmas.

Ceylon was still lovely and hot and we disembarked at Colombo, travelling by ancient cockroach-ridden train overnight up to the hills, where we rented a house for a month. It was a bungalow with rather primitive-type plumbing, serviced by 'Dan Dan the lavatory man', who called daily to empty the lavatories from the outside of the house. These I hasten to add were accessed by the inhabitants from indoors!

There were several servants who took charge of all domestic duties including babysitting – they all loved children. We visited our tea planter friends and spent a day with them exploring the plantation. We also visited the Botanic Gardens in Kandy, taking a local bus which drove along the desperately curly and bumpy and seemingly endless road, causing even me to feel car sick which I never normally am.

Ceylon was my first face-to-face encounter with leeches – the blood-sucking creatures; luckily less face-to-face, they crept into my shoes and attached themselves to my feet and ankles, and after taking their fill, disappeared. For some reason their presence was painless at the time, until removing one's shoes later when there was the gory evidence. Felicity was also attacked by one clinging to her leg but our host simply applied his fag end to it causing it to fall off – Felicity jumped in surprise as well.

It was interesting to examine at close quarters the whole hillside covered in tea bushes – *camellia sinensis* – which thrived happily in this lovely countryside. The tea was harvested by many local ladies who using both hands to cut the small shoots which grew annually on the tea bushes, and tossed them over their shoulders into a large bag, which they wore on their backs for the purpose.

The second half of our journey continued in another trooper, which picked us up at Colombo and included Christmas and

New Year – never have I had such a luxurious season with turkey and plum pudding, parties and presents all taken care of by the management. It really was a free holiday cruise and delivered us at Southampton as ready as possible to face the darkest time of the English winter, and our anxiety about Simon and what could be done to cope with the dire polio damage.

We decamped onto John's mother as usual, in Woking, Surrey, where his father had been vicar. Lottie adored her grandchildren and liked nothing better than being left to look after them. John had to report to the Admiralty to find out his next job and I had to find the best doctor for Simon. So we were extremely grateful to her.

The only doctor I knew was the GP who had looked after me when Martin was born just before we left for Singapore. He happened to know the surgeon, Mr Seddon, at the Royal Orthopaedic Hospital in London whose great expertise and life experience had been taking care of just such unusual cases as Simon. What a bit of luck.

Mr Seddon was the kindest cleverest man and took enormous trouble over Simon. At our first appointment there were several students who were all allowed to stand by while he was examined; Simon who had hardly any clothes on, complained slightly, not caring for this sort of attention. Mr Seddon quite understood and sent for a small dressing gown.

They all discussed what was the best way to treat Simon's problem and Mr Seddon decided to replace the paralysed muscle at the back of his neck, which he would make from fascia (a kind of muscular substance) taken from Simon's thigh; he would use this to join his skull to his spine, thus ensuring that he grew up straight. I could hardly believe such things were possible, but I had great faith in this amazing and imaginative expert and it was all arranged that Simon should enter the Royal Orthopaedic Hospital at Stanmore as soon as possible for this inventive procedure.

John went off to his new job in Plymouth, and my grandmother in Scotland invited Felicity and Martin to stay (I provided an au pair to accompany them).

Meanwhile I stayed with my sister, Anne – now a producer at the BBC – in London from where I could visit Simon every day.

She persuaded the BBC to give me an interview to see if I was suitable for any lowly occupation. My only experience at office work had been in the WRNS and after several attempts to take a speed typing test (I think I managed 29 words per minute), the kind girl asked if I could do better if I came back next day. I had to admit I could never do any better, so I was offered a job in the filing department. This I could manage and I was delighted to find that if you didn't take your morning coffee (10.30–11.00), your lunch (1–2pm) or your tea break (half an hour) time off, you could leave two hours early; so I was able to dash off to Simon's hospital not too far away. There my job was to keep him as stationary as possible, lying on his back while I read to him. The whole routine was no easy task and one day I fainted, which did not help matters. After that they insisted on giving me lunch every day.

Slowly Simon's condition improved and at last we were allowed home and his long convalescence began. From then on, we had to visit Mr Seddon every few months where he would always have students there to examine Simon's progress – and answer his questions: "Could he turn somersaults?" This was discussed at length with the students and later, at another consultation, it was decided he could – and play football, but not rugby!

Christian with her family on holiday in the 50s

LEAVING THE ROYAL NAVY

The several years during which I had 'followed the fleet', moving house every time John had a new appointment and having babies wherever we happened to be, were easy enough to begin with and one got very used to it. But after Singapore, it was time to think again.

With the Royal Navy being halved several times, there was little hope of a future with suitable promotions. John therefore decided to leave the service and while he was taking up his last appointment (which happened to be on an aircraft carrier based in Plymouth) he also started to job hunt.

We took a house in Downderry, in Cornwall, so John could commute daily to his aircraft carrier. There was a small school there, which suited our current needs. I would take the children every morning with Felicity bicycling, Simon tricycling (when he became fit enough) and Martin running behind. There was a cliff path down to the beach opposite our house, so we spent a lot of time climbing up and down and picnicking by the sea.

Anne and Johnnie were married by now and came to stay with us again which cheered us greatly. They had bought a house near Bristol and Anne had successfully manoeuvred her job at the BBC to the branch there where she could make the programmes she liked best.

She was rather good at radio programmes. She found more scope for these and one of her best was based on the subject of 'honesty'. She discovered a most interesting burglar during her research. During his interview he described how he never bought anything – he always stole everything. It seemed to be against his principles to pay for anything – but he did admit that he made an exception if he gave a present to his mother! Anne seemed to have a gift for finding interesting people, which stood her in good stead when she was asked to make *A Leap in the Dark*, her series about the occult.

We used to go and stay with Anne and Johnnie, which was always fun. Anne was a brilliant cook but she never managed to produce dinner much before bedtime. Fortunately, Johnnie would take over.

Johnnie had his foibles, one of which was that he hated spending too much, so when it came to Christmas and turkeys, he would always wait until late on Christmas Eve when they were almost giving the birds away, when he would rush home with his triumph!

Eventually, John was offered two jobs. One was something to do with rope in Glasgow, and the other was Harbourmaster in the port of Par in Cornwall which he decided to take. The harbour belonged to a big Cornish firm called English China Clays and seemed very busy shipping this much-in-demand product in small ships mostly to European customers.

The clay came from anywhere below the surface of Cornwall – you only had to start digging, it seemed, so there were many enormous clay pits. Par harbour was a tiny little port; it was tidal, which meant it dried out at every low tide, so ships could be seen anchoring off the coast during the shallow period, waiting to come alongside and load up with china clay.

Houses were few and far between and to begin with, we moved from Downderry and rented one in Fowey to get a feel of the neighbourhood. It had the most marvellous view of the river port and we joined the Yacht Club which was nearby. As luck would have it, Derek Edleston, our friend from Gibraltar days, had an aunt and godmother in Fowey so we had a flying start to our social life, which was a bit of luck.

We finally bought a house in Tywardreath, a village a few miles west of Fowey which had four bedrooms and was about the right size for our family. It had a small garden and was very much part of the village, with houses either side. Tywardreath had a post office, a pub and a rather beautiful old church. The house was to be found at the top of a hill which sloped down, passing Par station from where British Rail would take you to London in four hours.

Par was an unprepossessing straggly village which had been on the coast in days gone by, but now the sea had receded and left behind the harbour and quite a long sandy beach.

Felicity and Simon were starting boarding school and there was a place in a daily establishment for Martin close by. Our travels round the world living in other people's houses had resulted in us having very little furniture of our own, so we set about the local auction house, conveniently located in Par, to buy ourselves at minimum cost what we needed. It was a new experience for Martin and me – I would pick him up after school, we would go straight to the auction house, and having looked at what was on offer we would enjoy the indescribable excitement of bidding for our choice. A sofa and two chairs with new loose covers would go for something like £2! Martin got so keen on this method of trade that he would ask me eagerly, "How much would those carrots go for?" when we continued our shopping in the greengrocer.

We had also acquired a dog by this time. The children had longed for one when we were in Singapore, but it was not a good idea to have one out there for various reasons, so I promised them one when we got back to England.

We decided on a Dachshund as it had advantages – such as it was long enough for three children to pat it without fighting; it also had short hair and didn't need much upkeep. We found a black puppy – the most adorable creature you could imagine – and we called it Chipolata (small sausage) and she became known as Chippa. At the same time we indulged in a ginger kitten and the two became inseparable friends, playing endless games, though it was always the kitten who decided when to stop.

We were invited by John's firm to various social functions which were interesting. One was a sort of cocktail party where nobody introduced anybody – as I suppose they all knew each other – but where all the men occupied one end of the room and the women the other. We were invited to buy tickets for the local Christmas Ball at the Carlyon Bay hotel, where there was a prize given each year by a different trade. That year it was the local undertaker, so I suppose you could win a free funeral.

I must admit we felt rather out of our element.

MY EDUCATION

By the time Martin was old enough to go to boarding school I became very under-employed. I tried to get a job teaching French at the local school, but being fluent but unqualified, I failed.

I was horrified to find myself reading *War and Peace* in the morning. Something must be done. So I volunteered to help with some charities raising money for various ventures and met a neighbour of mine, Gillian Carlyon, who had also been a Wren during the war – a mutual bond.

Gillian was endeavouring to restore her enormous, 300-year-old garden which was full of fascinating plants introduced by her plant-collecting ancestors over the years.

Many years before, one of Gillian's ancestors had fallen in love with the coachman's daughter and ran away with her to New Zealand, newly discovered by Captain Cook. There the young man set up a sheep and cattle station, which eventually became one of the largest in the North Island. He also began laying out the skeleton of what would be a garden based on Tregrehan, the garden in his old home in Cornwall. He kept in touch with his family and the link between the two countries kept going. Gillian – the latest of these descendants – had been brought up in New Zealand and had only come to live in Cornwall when she was about 12 and her father inherited the estate. Now, with her parents having both died, it was left to her to update this huge property.

There were several hundred acres of garden at Tregrehan, not to mention the enormous house which needed a lot of maintenance. Gillian was an enterprising character and learnt from builders how to repair the roof, at which she became quite adept, but her main interest was the wonderful garden full of many plants which had been new introductions by her ancestors during the past centuries, some of whose labels had disappeared. These all had to be reidentified and she sent packages up to Kew Gardens on a regular basis.

I found her willing to have some unskilled but enthusiastic labour to help her with this project. Here was a wonderful opportunity for me to be useful and to learn so much about exciting and unusual plants.

Every day I was learning about interesting species I had never heard of, particularly camellias which will always be my favourite plant. They have so many unique qualities. To begin with they are evergreen with luscious shiny leaves throughout the year. There are many thousands of varieties with different coloured and formed flowers produced throughout the winter months – the earliest flower in October and the later ones continue until May – from white and every shade of pink to darkest red, some with stripes and other colour formations. There are bushes which are very upright growing and make good hedges and others have a flowing evening-dress habit sweeping elegantly to the ground.

At Tregrehan there were plantations of camellias in their many varieties. There were also avenues of rare trees, a walled garden in which delicate plants were better protected and a huge greenhouse filled with unusual plants and climbers from many countries, which could be heated if required. Evergreen lapagerias were to be found in here scrambling up the walls, with their huge bell-like flowers – red was the common one but there was also white and pale pink. They were named after Joséphine de la Pagerie, Napoleon's wife, who came from Martinique.

Gardening soon became my passionate mania and to know the history of each plant became my aim. I had to know who brought it back to Britain and where from and how did it all come about.

The years flew by. I must have bored everyone I knew about my new hobby, because one day a friend rang up and told me I must apply to join a magical course at the Open University called The Age of Enlightenment. It didn't specify particular information on plants, but I could tell it would open my mind to the whole background of that wonderful period of history – well and truly titled. So, at the age of 75, I returned to formal education and began a degree.

It was supposed to take only 15 hours a week; it took me double this and at the end I would have liked to have done the whole course again. This was not permitted however, so Ancient Greek was suggested instead. I knew there would not be room in my head for another enormous subject, so I continued my quest for botanical knowledge of this magical period in various libraries.

Kew Library was the best once you had discovered how to extract knowledge from this complicated source – it has now been rebuilt and computerised, if there is such a word.

Then there is the library at the Linnean Society, devoted to natural history of all sorts, and of course the Royal Horticultural Society Library which was also full of valuable information.

I discovered such people as Princess Augusta _ who was responsible for starting Kew Gardens – her son George III and his great friend (and my hero) Joseph Banks. I found out about Catherine the Great, who asked King George III for a selection of his rare plants from Kew. One can sense her enthusiasm as the plants arrived in St Petersburg at six in the morning – she was there to meet them and study the many varieties chosen for her. Later, as they flowered, Catherine appeared again at six in the morning, to paint the blooms when they came out.

From these libraries I was able to find original letters, articles and documents written by these historic people, from this marvellous Age of Enlightenment – now my favourite period of history.

My particular interest in Joseph Banks began when I discovered that he had accompanied Captain Cook in his round-the-world voyage as a botanist on HMS *Endeavour*, for which he paid his own expenses and those of his nine assistants. He was a rich young man and dedicated his time, money, brains and life to the furtherance of scientific knowledge, and botany in particular. On their return, King George III sent for him to hear of the voyage at first hand and it was thus that they became lifelong friends sharing their mutual interest in such matters. The King made him a baronet and appointed him unofficial director of the gardens at Kew.

I was very grateful to this university course because it had revealed to me so many subjects that I must follow up, and I badly needed the Oxford training I had missed out on so many years before.

Restoring the fascinating old garden at Tregrehan was quite expensive and although the estate was not penniless it was decided that the garden should pay its way. There was a square at the back of the house and from there several outbuildings spread out in decorative ways. These were furnished and decorated to be let as holiday flats. As for the garden, we thought a way of making it pay would be to establish a business selling camellia cuttings. It was quite a resourceful idea, but not necessarily easy. However, after a few false starts and encouraging some known potential customers, it began to take off. Because there were so many varieties of this species, we would get orders for several thousand specimens of one particular camellia. It was quite a lengthy business taking the cuttings, but they were easy to pack up and send off in polythene bags, and I was capable of helping the whole project. I must admit I got very involved with this time-consuming occupation, where I was learning and enjoying myself so much.

Tregrehan became quite well known and I remember an occasion where a customer came to visit this famous Cornish fount of camellia varieties and she dared, when she thought no one was watching, to dig up a plant and try to make off with it. By pure chance Gillian saw her and when the villain got into her car and took off, Gillian, who drove a Porsche, pursued her, made a citizen's arrest and took her to the police station!

There was another rather dramatic, but different and certainly memorable occasion, when one of the camellia customers invited Gillian to visit him in New York. She insisted on my coming with her because it would be so much more fun. So she booked two first-class return tickets to New York on the *QE2*, just for the day. It was a memorable experience. I remember the sight of the huge Statue of Liberty as we sailed past it at five in the morning, the pale pink morning light adding much to the experience – some other passengers who actually lived in New York were interested in our day trip, exclaiming that it would be quite long enough.

After our visit to Gillian's customer, there was time to drive round the city in a double sized limo, visiting Wall Street and other such famous places, on the way to the even more memorable Twin Towers. I will never forget the lift which carried you up to the extraordinary altitude; it could accommodate perhaps a hundred people. When it took off, the speed with which you shot up the shaft left most of yourself behind. I have never flown in a lift of such calibre.

Lunch had been booked at the smartest club in the Twin Towers. I seem to remember I had caviar with delicious blinis. It was amazing to look down and see the whole of New York – especially when you recollect now, how you could never, ever see it again.

Then it was time to make our way back to the *QE2*, waiting patiently for us to return in such luxury to England.

MY GARDEN

At the end of this wonderful period, Gillian sadly died and Tregrehan was inherited by her nephew, a lucky young man in his twenties who came over from New Zealand to take it on.

I could no longer play in this fairyland and so resolved to make use of the large amount of knowledge I had gleaned from the experience and dedicate my time to my own much smaller garden of about a third of an acre. There was enough space for our children to play French cricket and the garage end quickly filled up with bicycles and bits of John's boat that needed attention.

It was to be the first time I had ever had the opportunity of creating a garden and I intended to clear the uninteresting flower-beds and extend the lawn, making a *tabula rasa* for my plans.

Tregrehan had been full of the most unusual and exotic plants, introduced over the years, some with their original lead labels still attached. I would acquire as many of these interesting and historic varieties as I could find, that were not too big, and fill my garden with them.

The property was in the middle of the village and the garden was already enclosed by an old stone wall on one side. I thought of surrounding the rest of it with camellia hedges, which would give me a luscious evergreen enclosure, with ravishing flowers from the many different varieties which flower between October and May. The beautiful old wall, about 10 feet high, would be perfect for the many climbing plants I had in mind and as protection for some of the more delicate species I would try to grow.

The property consisted of a long narrow plot, with the house – which had an early Victorian look about it – in the middle and facing south. I intended to divide the whole into three parts: the west which sloped down to the road where shade was provided by a large conker tree; the eastern section would be marked with a myrtle hedge and a small archway through it to allow access for the path towards the garage.

Opposite the house were two large and well-established palm trees –*Trachycarpus fortunei* – which I would allow to remain and which, with the conker tree, were the only items in the whole garden not chosen and grown by me. They would mark the southern boundary and join the camellia hedges as barriers.

Against the east wall of the house was a rather battered greenhouse. Inside it grew a moribund vine which had no place in my plans. I replaced it with a new metal greenhouse, outside which I placed a square stone terrace which would be ideal for picnics and sitting in the sun; this was surrounded by a balustrade for different exciting climbers.

Among the many varieties of Camellia, I chose a very upright growing *C. Japonica x 'E.G. Waterhouse'* (named after the Australian professor of that name), which had particularly elegant pink formal double flowers, for the hedge opposite the house, which would divide the property from the house next door. Where it ended, by the myrtle coming from the opposite direction, I extended it with a camellia hedge of many varieties which joined it to the garage end of the demesne. In the corner where the two hedges met, I planted two spreading camellias *C. Japonica 'Sabina'* which is a pretty double white with an occasional pink stripe and *C. Japonica 'Lady Clare'*, a deep pink large bloom, which would spread out their evergreen foliage downwards like a coloured fringe.

I greatly enjoyed improving my garden in various ways and found it an unending source of interest, requiring endless trips to various gardens or libraries to add to my knowledge. Not to mention my various expeditions abroad. Gardening in Cornwall does become a considerable mania, partly because you can grow almost anything in the county, where all plants love the climate, and where, as I have said many times, it rarely stops raining.

John loved Cornwall and spent his leisure time sailing – joining the Royal Fowey Yacht Club and taking his boat out in our unreliable climate, quite happily.

However, I personally do not care for endless rain and found I had to go abroad at least once a year to enjoy some really boiling, boiling sunshine; I found January was the best time for this, when little needed to be done to my garden and I could take off to investigate some obscure plant I was interested in.

I would usually go by sea and found a very splendid girl who had been employed on cruises and she would find me what I wanted – a small ship, to go where the plant I was investigating grew, always in

January. In plenty of time she would give me a choice of voyage, so I could research all I needed to know before going.

I joined the International Dendrology Society, which often went on the sort of expedition I enjoyed, though not usually by sea. I went to Thailand with the Dendros (as I called them) and Belize, followed by Delhi and the Himalayas which taught me a great deal. I could actually see Mount Everest from where we were staying. I also joined the International Camellia Society and followed them round parts of China, thus adding to my interest.

The years went by without one noticing – suddenly I was 80! John was older than me and sadly died in 1999. We had managed a few cruises together after he retired, but now I was on my own and thankful for my obsession, which kept me busy.

It was at this point that I invented a lecture on Sir Joseph Banks.

Never having given a lecture in my life, I was persuaded by a friend that any fool could lecture – all you needed was a good beginning and a good end because (she said) no one ever listens to anything in the middle. So I started inventing such a talk on camellias, about which I know something; after all my interesting discoveries about Banks, I thought this marvellous man, so fascinating and so little known, would make another subject for my collection.

It was a particularly good moment as his 'Grand and Stylish publication' was at last printed in colour, under the aegis of the Natural History Museum, as a limited edition of 110 sets with 723 prints in each; the specialist printers at Historical Alecto were kind enough to give me a selection of slides, which illustrated the making of these brilliant prints, and I acquired a list of the purchasers of the collections. I chose half a dozen of these illustrious names, partly for where they were located (I particularly wanted to go to California to see the redwoods), but also for the least intimidating institutions, and wrote a carefully worded letter, suggesting that they might like to hear my lecture on their magnificent purchase.

I was thrilled to receive an invitation to the Filoli Center in Woodside near San Francisco, and another to address a banquet at Redwood City. Using these as a lever I managed to arrange three more dates with the Garden Club of America. I nervously decided to accept everything – if I couldn't lecture before I went, I would certainly be a dab hand by my return.

Having filled so many notebooks with interesting information, I thought I might write a book. I did not know how to set about this, but I already had a sort of word processor so asked the advice of my neighbour, Mike Phillips, who seemed to know about such things. I didn't realise until much later that Mike was a magic man in just this sort of expertise. He found me a second-hand machine and taught me to use it. I was extremely stupid and took some time to absorb the minimum which would enable me to start writing my book.

It was about then that Mike said he didn't want to be paid any more as he enjoyed what I asked him to do. So, I asked him what he drank and he said mostly gin. So I decided to keep him in gin for the foreseeable future.

There didn't seem to be any rules about writing books so I just plunged in as if I was telling a story. I thought I could improve the beginning when I had something substantial to add to it. I went on like this from day to day, really quite enjoying the whole experience.

BACK TO LONDON

Eventually I decided, rather on the spur of the moment, to move myself and the best of my belongings from Cornwall back to London. My by now large family found it very difficult to visit me from the various parts of the UK where they lived and although I didn't often think about it, I was getting older. So I asked Felicity, my daughter, if she could find me a flat near the river in London. She immediately set about looking for me and within a year found me the perfect answer to my prayer.

I felt quite different becoming once more a resident in London. To begin with, not having a car any more was a tremendous loss of independence. My beloved BMW was my companion for 15 years and being without it felt like the loss of a friend. But it is no good having a car in London, as the only time you really want it is when you want to go beyond the city's limits. So, you become a Londoner with your sights firmly fixed on buses or taxis. I am too old for undergrounds. Fortunately, not only does my magic flat overlook the River Thames, but on the other side of a roundabout in front of the house is a staircase which leads you directly (provided you have a key to the gate) to the bus stop from where you can travel to most parts of London.

I discovered that the buses were, amazingly, much the same (even their numbers) as they used to be when I lived in London during the war, so I found no difficulty in taking myself to my hairdresser in Sloane Square, my dentist in Knightsbridge and other necessary neighbours. I could actually walk to church just across the river – Mass every Sunday – so I was more or less at home.

An enormous treat that I had not often been able to indulge in while living in Cornwall was the Proms. I have always been a passionate lover of classical music, learning the piano at school and always having a small gramophone with me, which played all my favourite records – Bach, Handel, Beethoven, Mozart, Vivaldi and so on. At home I could never practise the piano, because following the fleet, as we always did, there never seemed to be a piano where we happened to be living; my gramophone came with me wherever I went, however.

Sure enough when I got to London, there were the Proms, my favourite sort of entertainment, and an amazing stroke of luck pointed me to the choir about to perform Handel's *Messiah* at the Albert Hall just before Christmas. I met a lady who sang every year in this heavenly production and she asked me if I would like to join. I had belonged to my school choir and also the Bach choir when I was becoming an officer in the Wrens at Greenwich, but I couldn't believe I could possibly be accepted. However, my friend said there were two permanent professional choirs and they took on about 50 extras at festival times. I rushed to the little music shop in South Kensington and bought a copy of the score.

"Ring them up," my friend said, "and tell them you want to join." She gave me the number and, to my amazement, they agreed.

We went together to all the rehearsals where luckily it was always the sopranos who were more at fault than the altos (my range), who were luckily less obtrusive.

There were to be two performances two days running just before Christmas, and we had to take a picnic to the Albert Hall basement where a huge room was filled with choir members. You were lucky to find a hook on the wall to hang your bag on, let alone a chair to sit on.

I had many times sat in the audience side of this enormous hall, but it was such a privilege to be on the stage side – with all the soloists in front of one it was thrilling. It was one of the grandest experiences of my life, and one that I believe I will never forget. I placed myself next to a girl with a stunning soprano voice, so I could be unobtrusive but yet enjoy myself. I think I enjoyed the second night even more because I knew what to expect and had a more favourable seat.

Living in London, of course, there was no way I could replace my garden, but I have the Chelsea Physic Garden nearby and on my little balcony I have two potted-up camellias and a climber, a lapageria, which I hope are happy.

One other enormous and unexpected plus was when my Cornish friend Liz Fortescue told me she had a daily help for me. In no time Maria, a splendid Portuguese lady who Liz had known for over 20 years, came to take charge of my every household need. It seemed all too good to be true.

However, at this moment, fate took a hand in my proceedings and, while spending Easter with Felicity in her house in Berkshire, I fell backwards down her stairs and cracked a great many bones.

The 10 days I spent in hospital made me realise how helpless I was, but also that the amazing technical staff had to do everything for me. I could not get over how many nice-looking young men seemed to be looking after such helpless patients as me. I had to ask them how they could bring themselves to do the sort of revolting things they had to do. Wiping people's bottoms? They giggled and said when you spent your life doing things like that a hundred times a day, you hardly noticed it! They were all so kind and jolly and capable as well – it made you feel better.

Then came the moment when Felicity and I had to decide what to do with me next. There was a part of the hospital that specialised in helping my sort of problem, but we decided that as I was longing to go home, that would be best – with only one proviso. I would have to have a live-in carer, at a price, who would be provided by Universal Aunts, the remarkable agency which produces such people.

Could I afford such luxury? After a great deal of thought and discussion, Felicity and Simon said they thought I could afford to stay in my flat for eight years. Hoping very much to be dead long before that(!), I went home.

Luckily I can't remember the next few weeks but when a physio called Harriet was sent to treat me, she said everything I had been doing up to that date had been making me worse! Now she would give me exercises which I must do every half hour, and she would come back in a fortnight to see how I was progressing. She did just that and although I struggled to do as she told me (every half hour was a bit extreme, I thought) I did the exercises as often as I could – and to my surprise when Harriet came again she was impressed by the progress I had made. I could not see it myself, but the pain was if anything slightly less.

Then Harriet decided that I must have a special chair, whose sole purpose it seemed to me was to be as uncomfortable as possible. When it came, she measured it to fit me and we put it by the window, looking over the river, and strangely if I sat straight in it, it wasn't so bad. Then Harriet said I must do the stairs; she was quite right as otherwise I would be marooned upstairs. Although I trembled at that, Harriet knows what she is doing and after a few expeditions I could just about manage tentatively. Harriet decided that to be safe I must have a second hand bar on the wall side of the stairs – in no time she had met with no objections from the other residents, and a young man arrived to carry out the work for the NHS. The wooden handrail he put up – to Harriet's measurements – was perfection and gave me enormous confidence as I climbed my way up and down (twice) every day.

Now that I could do the stairs safely, with my carer in charge, I did my exercises every morning and started to go out for a walk in the gardens before lunch. Harriet also arranged for a strange vehicle, which I christened 'the rotovator', with four wheels and a seat in the middle. My carer and I went out every morning, rain or shine, to explore the nearby gardens which have been carefully planned and have a very colourful selection of shrubs and plants round the several large lawns which surround the house and flats.

These all have balconies and windows which add to the delightful gardens. There are benches here and there, too, and when it is sunny we sit out among them.

Harriet said she could not do any more for me and so, she said goodbye!

KEEPING THE MARBLES AFLOAT

On my 95th birthday, I came round after surgery for a new hip, to find that my daughter had sent a concise email report to some members of the family who might be interested:

"Operation OK – marbles intact."

This may have been a slight exaggeration at the time but reassured those concerned.

More than five years later, how to preserve these precious marbles is of great concern. I continue with my daily fitness regime. Though there are mornings when I would rather stay in bed, I feel an obligation – as an admiral's daughter perhaps – to take care of my health to the best of my ability. I play bridge, I read about everything and anything that interests me, and I have written four books since I was 80. I write about plants and their histories. But there is no doubt that my marbles are not what they were. I find that not only am I liable to forget people's names – I was never very good at their faces anyway, being very short-sighted, but much more serious is forgetting the names of my precious plants. Now that I don't walk past them every day, I have to keep looking them up in my book – where I wrote about them – and see what I said.

One is led to believe that long-term memory is not such a problem as day-to-day happenings, thus it is important to check in your address book so that you know who is still around. This fact is further rubbed in when your friends reach the considerable age of 90 or so and repeat themselves to you. I may say that my address book is now full of names I cannot recognise.

I read *The Times* every day, that is to say I skim through the news headlines, read further details of anything that appeals, get to the hatches, matches and despatches and any aspects of the obituaries – occasionally referring to people I have known or heard of, describing parts of their lives that are new to me. *The Spectator* comes every Friday – in theory at least, but the post is so unreliable that I cannot count on it. The contributors to this weekly newspaper vary but I have my favourites and these take some concentration.

Playing bridge is one of the most important occupations towards the preservation of my marbles. It is the only academic game worth playing in my opinion – always a challenge, never the same twice. I go to the Andrew Robson Club occasionally and find it a great treat to play with total strangers picked at random, who may from time to time not be one's preferred choice. On the other hand, I have found this spurs me on and I play more than usually well. Great self-control is required when one's partner (for the game) does something particularly idiotic, but their forbearance is expected when you make a similar mistake. One tries to remember that at my age nothing gets better and will inevitably get worse. So here goes slowing the process down.

Becoming 100 years old seems to be something of an achievement. It happened so suddenly. The last few years I seem to have been so busily occupied – writing, lecturing and then taking up painting with my Estonian friend Anna – I could hardly believe it when Felicity told me she had started making plans for my 100th birthday party!

At my daughter's suggestion, formal invitations were sent out to my many descendants to a garden party in her Berkshire home, and more to friends to indulge at my riverside flat the next day in London.

The latter was a tea party – starting at 5 o'clock and involving anyone who had been unable to come to the other parties. And, of course, the cake! This was a total surprise, given to me by the firm of Searcy's of Sloane Street, who had made my wedding cake in 1943 at my mother's request. The managing director brought the huge, beautiful cake to my flat to present it at the party – nothing better could have celebrated the day.

Thinking back over 100 years is quite an ordeal. I have run through most of the physical changes as they came and went, but what about the developments in my person? If I could be the judge of these, what would I notice?

I suppose I altered from a juvenile when I joined the Wrens; that was the first time that I made all my own decisions. Escaping from Miss Buckmaster was certainly under my own steam. Again, choosing plotting over coding was inspired and influenced the rest of my career and steered me towards first of all Plymouth and all those wonderful submariners, and then to Belfast and my husband John, the most important of my decisions. After that, decisions were mostly taken between us both. But after John died I was a different person – a rather bereft person, no longer making my own decisions but used to talking things over before deciding. Now I was truly on my own and it was not a pleasant place to be. Rock bottom one used to say – but this was reality.

Having reached 100 years I decided it was time to look forward again – and one must have a goal – but without any experience of 100 plus, how could one begin? Well, I will tell you how I began and that was to make sure that everything I chose to do must be enjoyable. Previously everything such as duty, cost, other people's feelings and tastes and other outside values would have come first – now it was only selfish me that was going to count, and what would my goal be?

What I like doing best is having a project such as a book I want to write, with a laptop which behaves as I order it, and where the research needed for such a project is to hand. I also enjoy the sort of things that Simon Robinson, my friend who is trying to make me famous, arranges for me in the way of enjoyable interviews with magic people like Dan Snow (who describes me in the only programme I have done with him as a heroine!), and who also thinks up things I have never envisioned and plans them for me.

Then there is meeting either old friends to play bridge or new interesting people, and now I come to think of it any new suggestions which I have never contemplated before. There are also completely new and exciting things I can't imagine, which before being 100 would not have been possible! Where are they and what are they?

So here goes. The foreseeable future is full of possibilities that are new to any 100-year-old and I can't wait for them to begin.

101st birthday here I come!

ACKNOWLEDGEMENTS

There are many people to whom I owe a debt of gratitude upon the publication of this book.

Firstly, I want to thank my friends and fellow Wrens for their contributions, sent in response to a request I made several years ago when researching my self-published book, *I Only Joined For The Hat.* I'm delighted to be bringing their stories to a wider audience at last. In alphabetical order: Catherine Avent, Daphne Baker, Mary Brown, Mary Earl, Jane Fawcett, Joy Hale, Priscilla Hext, Mary Hilton Jones, Sister Pamela Hussey, Hope Maclean, Monica McConnell, Hazel Russell, Elizabeth Duchess of Northumberland and Mary Wynn-Jones. I'm also grateful to have been able to include wartime letters from my late friend Lennox Napier DSO DSC, Captain of HMS *Rorqual.*

Thanks are also due to Chris Manby, Mike Phillips, Simon Robinson, Jamie Rollo, Laurence Cole and Jo Sollis for their various roles in helping to prepare my manuscript, and to my son Simon John Lamb for his work around his father's memoir.

Most importantly, I wish to thank my husband Lieutenant Commander John Bruce Lamb DSC, RN, extracts of whose own naval memoir, *Tales of the Last Dog Watch*, are published herein.

Christian Lamb
June 2021

"On my balcony with a beautiful view of the river Thames" 2021

Christian Lamb is the daughter of an admiral, who herself became a Wren, then a naval wife. A passionate plantswoman with a particular interest in camellias, she is a Fellow of the Linnean Society & member of the Dendrology Society. A well-respected lecturer on the history of plants, she has written extensively about the world's most notable botanic gardens and is an authority on the English naturalist Sir Joseph Banks (1743–1820).

INDEX

Y